SpringerBriefs in Intelligent Systems

Artificial Intelligence, Multiagent Systems, and Cognitive Robotics

This series covers the entire research and application spectrum of intelligent systems, including artificial intelligence, multiagent systems, and cognitive robotics. Typical texts for publication in the series include, but are not limited to, state-of-the-art reviews, tutorials, summaries, introductions, surveys, and in-depth case and application studies of established or emerging fields and topics in the realm of computational intelligent systems. Essays exploring philosophical and societal issues raised by intelligent systems are also very welcome.

Harshit Mishra · Sucheta Soundarajan

Addressing Bias
in Information Retrieval

Springer

Harshit Mishra
Department of Electrical Engineering
and Computer Science
Syracuse University
Syracuse, NY, USA

Sucheta Soundarajan
Department of Electrical Engineering
and Computer Science
Syracuse University
Syracuse, NY, USA

ISSN 2196-548X   ISSN 2196-5498 (electronic)
SpringerBriefs in Intelligent Systems
ISBN 978-3-032-24144-3   ISBN 978-3-032-24145-0 (eBook)
https://doi.org/10.1007/978-3-032-24145-0

This Springer imprint is published by the registered company Springer Nature Switzerland AG
The registered company address is: Gewerbestrasse 11, 6330 Cham, Switzerland

If disposing of this product, please recycle the paper.

To those who try to make the world better.

Preface

Information Retrieval (IR) systems are an important part of the modern world. They facilitate the discovery of relevant content and surround us in the form of recommender systems, web-based search engines, digital libraries, and feed-based social media platforms. Rapid advancements in the field of IR have transformed how we interact with the world around us, so much so that the world without the IR systems seems antiquated.

In this book, we observe that not *all* such advancements have been good for *all*. The processes involved in building IR systems, such as data collection, training data, and algorithmic models, are not without fault. They exist in a society that has continuously struggled with prejudices and discrimination, which are reflected throughout the entire IR process. We make a case for why one should care for biases in IR systems, and then, understanding the importance of the systems, provide ways to quantify and mitigate the unfairness and make such systems *good* for all.

The goal of this book is to encourage readers to look beyond the relevance and fairness tradeoffs and to discuss the impact that an unfair IR system can have on its end users, while also providing methods to make information retrieval systems good for *all*.

Both authors were supported by the U.S. National Science Foundation Award # 2047224.

Syracuse, USA Harshit Mishra
August 2025 Sucheta Soundarajan

Contents

Chapter 1
Introduction

Abstract Information retrieval refers to the task of finding material from a large corpus, usually stored on computers, to satisfy an information need. In this chapter, we trace the history of the field of information retrieval—from Vannevar Bush's Memex device to today's digital technologies. We discuss four phases of the history of information retrieval, culminating in today's era of LLMs. We additionally describe metrics to evaluate information retrieval methods and systems. We conclude with a discussion of bias in information retrieval systems and ways in which information retrieval systems may cause harm.

1.1 Information Retrieval

Human advancement is closely linked to producing, archiving, and accessing relevant information. From oral traditions and stone tablets to modern websites and social media posts, the information that we generate produces a snapshot of the society at a given time. Information retrieval systems access the produced knowledge and deliver information relevant to the user's needs.

The Memex device proposed by Vannevar Bush in 1945 laid the conceptual foundation of many of today's IR systems. Bush envisioned a mechanized device that could store all books, records, and communications, and provide access to all recorded information with great speed, supplementing the user's memory [1]. The vision of storing and making human knowledge accessible finds its direct application today in digital libraries. The vast digital resources, including articles, books, and audio-visual media, are available to the global audience at an ever faster speed with the help of the Internet.

Information Retrieval (IR) as a field originated from library science. Early techniques focused on rule-based systems like Boolean retrieval and vector-based models [2–7]. In their current form they have transformed into recommender systems such as those used by Netflix, Amazon, Spotify, and YouTube, web-based search engines like Google and Bing, and chat-bots like ChatGPT and Gemini [8, 9]. Rapid development of data and digital technologies has influenced the information retrieval

© The Author(s), under exclusive license to Springer Nature Switzerland AG 2026
H. Mishra and S. Soundarajan, *Addressing Bias in Information Retrieval*,
SpringerBriefs in Intelligent Systems, https://doi.org/10.1007/978-3-032-24145-0_1

methods to evolve, to keep up with and efficiently handle the large scale of today's information.

Certain IR systems, such as recommender systems, extract and analyze user behavior data to predict which content will be most helpful and engaging for the users, and perform the important work of filtering down a large amount of content to a manageable chunk, which is then recommended to the user as suggestions. Other IR methods, such as web search engines, crawl and index all possible content on the web and deliver relevant information in response to a user's query. The methods differ, but the fundamental goal remains the same, Manning et al. define the task of information retrieval as follows [5]:

Information retrieval (IR) is the task of finding material (usually documents) of an unstructured nature (usually text) that satisfies an information need from within large collections (usually stored on computers).

Information retrieval systems that work on a large scale, processing vast amounts of data to serve users globally and provide relevant answers to communities with diverse cultures and histories, may face potential pitfalls that both users and developers of such systems should recognize. These systems may return results that over- or under-represent certain perspectives, often reflecting historical biases or perpetuating existing stereotypes [10–13].

Modern IR systems perform the task of indexing online information to fulfill their mission of delivering relevant information to the user. In that pursuit, they are also susceptible to capturing (and amplifying) existing harmful societal biases present in the world. If left unchecked, these systems can return harmful, biased results to users.

The evolution of information retrieval systems can be traced to the evolution of information. As methods to produce information changed over time, so did the methods of consuming relevant information.

Millennia-old methods such as cataloguing schemes were used to index books or papers, evolved into mechanical devices such as punched cards, which provided faster methods for manual scanning of the catalog. The advent of computers established Information Retrieval as a formal field of study [14].

We identify four main phases of evolution of modern information systems.

The **first** phase began with the advent of computers; IR researchers were limited to a small group of people, including librarians and paralegals, who specialized in information retrieval in the analog world. Such people were assigned the role of managing it in digital spaces.

The **second** phase was the web era. When the Internet became accessible in homes during the early 1990s, it triggered an explosive growth in information produced and consumed through platforms such as websites, search engines, and blogs.

The **third** phase was the social media era. Built on the web of the 1990s, social media provided a way for individual users to be visible to a global audience. This era included the development of household-name platforms such as Facebook, Instagram, and Reddit. The information here moved from closed forums to social networks and then to social platforms. This also marked the transition to platforms with fewer or no editorial responsibilities, disseminating information to their vast audience.

Unlike editorial sites such as newspapers, where only a limited few individuals can be creators, social media platforms blurred the lines, where the users of the platform can be simultaneously consumers as well as producers of the platform.

The **fourth** and current phase is of the post-GPT-4 LLMs era, where search has become conversational. Instead of providing a ranked list of documents to fulfill a user's query, the systems such as chat-bots rely on infrastructure developed in the third phase and use it to deliver a snippet of information, which is drawn from a set of relevant documents.

In the following sections, we describe the different methods of information retrieval that form the heart of different IR systems. The methods and evaluation measures discussed in this section are responsible for delivering relevant information to users.

1.1.1 Boolean Retrieval Model

In this section, we describe retrieval systems in which users build queries using precise language and retrieve documents that match the query. We use an example to illustrate how Boolean retrieval systems work.

Suppose that we have a collection of documents including:

1. John had a pizza and a soda for lunch.
2. Adam had a cheeseburger and soda for lunch.
3. John had a cheeseburger and lemonade for dinner.

Suppose that we wish to find the documents that contain the words soda AND cheeseburger. We can achieve this by linearly scanning each document and marking documents that contain the words 'soda' and 'cheeseburger'. Linear scanning is effective for a small number of documents, but the process becomes slows as the number of documents and size of documents increase. To avoid linear scanning, we construct a term-document incidence matrix. This involves collecting terms from each document as index terms and creating a vector for each term, which shows if the term appears in a document or not. Once documents are indexed, the incidence matrix provides faster ways to retrieve information. The rows of the matrix represents a vector for each term and the columns gives a vector for each document in terms of the words present in the corpus. To quickly scan a large collection of documents, one can use Boolean operators such as AND, OR, and NOT for fast retrieval. Moving forward with the example, we can create a term-document matrix as follows (Table 1.1).

To answer the query soda AND cheeseburger, we take the vectors of soda and cheeseburger, then do a bitwise AND:

$$110 \text{ AND } 011 = 010$$

Table 1.1 A term-document incidence matrix

Terms	Document 1	Document 2	Document 3
John	1	0	1
Pizza	1	0	0
Soda	1	1	0
Lunch	1	1	0
Adam	0	1	0
Cheeseburger	0	1	1
Lemonade	0	0	1
Dinner	0	0	1

The answer to this query is the set containing only Document 2. In the Boolean retrieval model, we formulate queries in Boolean expressions using AND, OR, and NOT. The system then retrieves documents that precisely match the query.

In the Boolean model, the user is responsible for formalizing a query, and if successful, all documents that match the query are returned as the result. This set may be too small or too large for the users needs, depending on the query and the collection of documents that can be retrieved. There was a need to consider documents that partially match the query as well as to score documents based on their relevance to the query.

1.1.2 Vector Space Models

Boolean retrieval returns documents that exactly match the query. When dealing with a large corpus of documents, such as indexing all the medical papers present on the web, it can lead to the system returning a quantity of documents that is impossible for a human to evaluate for their information needs [5]. Thus, because the Boolean model was too limiting for the delivery of relevant information to users [3, 4], automatic text retrieval systems were proposed as an alternative model [6]. In this model, each document is indexed with terms, and content identifiers are extracted from the user's query. Then, using a similarity measure, documents that meet the user's information need are returned as results to the user.

Salton and Buckley used vectors to represent documents and queries [7]. Using the index or content identification terms for each document, we can represent a document **D** by term vectors as

$$\mathbf{D} = (t_i, t_j, \ldots, t_p), \tag{1.1}$$

where each t_k is a term assigned to identify a document **D**. Similarly, we extract content identifier terms q_j from a query and define query **Q** as:

$$\mathbf{Q} = (q_a, q_b, \ldots, q_r). \tag{1.2}$$

Another way to formulate document and query vectors is similar to the example shown in Table 1.1. Each term in the database is assigned a binary indicator (1 or 0) indicating its presence in the document or query. Using this representation and a similarity measure, we can find documents relevant to the user's query. We measure a similarity value by comparing each vector index in the document and query vectors:

$$sim(\mathbf{Q}, \mathbf{D}) = \sum_{k=1}^{t} \mathbf{D_k} \cdot \mathbf{Q_k}, \tag{1.3}$$

where document $\mathbf{D_k}$ and query $\mathbf{Q_k}$ are represented as t-dimensional vectors.

Because each term in a document vector is assigned a binary value (0 or 1), common words present in multiple documents receive the same weight *1* as rarer, more distinctive terms. When processing search queries, we may wish to prioritize documents that assign greater weight to less frequent terms while reducing the influence of common terms that appear across many documents. To improve retrieval effectiveness, we may use an alternative approach to assign a variable weight to terms in a document: we assign a lower weight to a term that is present in all the documents and a higher weight to a term that is specific to few documents $\mathbf{D}$. By assigning non-binary weights to vector terms, we develop a partial matching framework [15]. We can also use a normalized weight assignment–e.g., cosine measure– to find a degree of similarity between a query and a document:

$$sim(\mathbf{Q}, \mathbf{D}) = \mathbf{D} \cdot \mathbf{Q}/|\mathbf{D}| * |\mathbf{Q}|, \tag{1.4}$$

where $|\mathbf{D}|$ and $|\mathbf{Q}|$ are the norms of the document and query vectors. The SMART retrieval system used the cosine similarity measure to evaluate IR systems [6].

If the weight of a term in a vector can vary from 0 to +1, then $sim(\mathbf{Q}, \mathbf{D})$ also varies between 0 and +1. Unlike the Boolean model, where we predict if a document is relevant to a query or not, here, we can rank the document according to the degree of similarity to the query.

We refer to [2, 5] for detailed experiments and evaluation of vector space models. We also refer to [16, 17] for a discussion on the mathematical basis for treating documents and queries in the same vector spaces.

1.1.3 Web Information Retrieval

The publicly available World Wide Web provided people a way to produce and consume information at a scale never seen before [18, 19]. By the late 1990s, the Web had more than a billion pages, rapidly transforming how people access information.

Changing user behavior with the advent of the web provided an interconnected web to navigate and find information. This behavior marked a departure from the sequential and limited way to retrieve information that was popular since the advent of computers [2, 20].

Changing user behavior: Before the World Wide Web, information production and consumption was costly. As the scale of documents grew, user behavior with respect to IR also changed, as users began to *browse* the web without a clear information need. **Browsing** refers to a user exploring the document space in front of them without asking a specific query to the system [2]. In traditional **searching**, the user has a clear goal in mind, whereas in **browsing**, the user has vague, unclear information needs. The system needed to adapt and facilitate *browsing* by learning user behavior, user search history, and documents available to the system. The system still needed to handle traditional, precise ways for IR, along with the modern vague information retrieval.

Flat Browsing: Here, the user doesn't have a clear information need [2]. They explore a set of documents retrieved by using a general query, for example, "European history". Then, the IR system observes user behavior and time spent on a web page, and suggests related pages that are similar to pages the user has visited in the current session. The systems also use query reformulation methods to make user queries better and continue to show more web pages, which can help satisfy users' information needs.

Structure guided Browsing: IR systems also need to satisfy traditional search strategies where a user searches for a label or an index that classifies a set of documents. Consider accessing a digital library to retrieve information about a topic. At the first level, the system may present a list of relevant books in the library. The next level of browsing could involve selecting among the chapters within a retrieved book, and the final level would provide access to the text itself. Here, hierarchically, the user explores a smaller set of documents. This is similar to finding an article on a news web page or reading an electronic book [2].

The Hypertext Model: Hypertexts were an important addition to the web space. As mentioned earlier, user behavior changed from satisfying sequential, precise information needs to exploration and browsing, where a user moves from one document/ page to another page to learn more information about a topic. This led to the formation of hypertexts [2, 21, 22]. Similar to references or bibliography at the end of a book, hypertexts referred the reader to another source that deals with a certain section in more detail. A web page could link to another web page and a user could navigate between them [23]. Similar to directed edges on a graph, where each node is a web page and a directed edge is present if a node has a hypertext link that navigates to another node.

As the web continued to evolve in a disorderly manner, finding information on the web became increasingly difficult. This led to the invention of search engines such as Yahoo, Alta Vista, and Google. Their main role was to explore existing web pages and return the most useful pages to the user [24–26].

1.1.3.1 Crawling

A major step in bringing order to the web was the creation of a crawler. From a set of starting pages, a crawler recursively collects pages by navigating to links mentioned in the pages. A crawler may assign an importance score to each page, and crawl pages based on this importance score [26–28]. Alternatively, a crawler may decide to crawl new pages first to maximize the freshness of the pages in the index [29, 30].

The order in which hypertexts are traversed determines the properties of the gathered collection. A crawler can traverse in a breadth-first manner, where it visits all the pages mentioned in the starting page before moving to their links, and so on, creating a wide but shallow collection. Alternatively, it can explore pages in a narrow depth-first manner, where it follows the first link on a starting page, then the first link on the subsequent page, and continues until no further links can be followed, creating a narrow but deep collection of webpages.

Once, the crawler has collected a set of documents, we need to create data structures to efficiently query the data. This leads to the creation of an inverted index, vocabulary, a URL database, a graph representation, and other data structures.

Document IDs are used to efficiently store and index the pages. Indexing facilitates a graph representation, where each document becomes a node and directed edges connect nodes when a document contains hyperlinks to others [31]. To better answer a user's query, a good indexer may also collect related pages to create a slightly bigger pool of similar documents [32].

1.1.3.2 Query Processor

Given a query, a query processor ranks documents in decreasing order of value to the user [25]. A numerical score is assigned to each document. The score combines two factors, a *query independent* factor that assesses document size, trust/ reputation, publication data; and a connectivity score, often evaluated using algorithms like PageRank [24, 26]. A *query dependent* factor which measures precision, recall, and cosine similarity, is then computed, taking both the query and the document into account [6].

1.1.3.3 Clustering

Clustering refers to grouping similar documents for better information retrieval [18, 33, 34]. Given a large database, it is inefficient to score each document. Clustering groups the documents and a search engine algorithm assigns scores to a set of documents that are deemed relevant to the user's query.

1.1.4 Collaborative Filtering

The web enables users to access content at exceedingly fast speeds and, in many cases, provides mechanisms for users to give feedback on content they have engaged with. Platforms such as Netflix and Amazon allow users to express likes or dislikes for items with a single click. This user feedback helps developers infer user interests and preferences, enabling platforms to deliver more relevant content.

Collaborative filtering is a type of model used by recommender systems that combines ratings and feedback left by users on the platform. This collaborative analysis helps platforms learn user interests over time and recommend content that may be relevant to each user. Consider two users, A and B, whose platform behavior shows they have engaged with very similar content and provided similar feedback. This pattern allows the platform to recommend an item x to user B if user A has already engaged with that item and provided positive feedback [35].

1.1.5 Content-Based Filtering

Content-based filtering methods recommend items based on user and item characteristics. Consider a user A who has left positive feedback on a collection of animated movies. Content-based recommendation algorithms can infer user preferences from their platform history and recommend an item x if it aligns with the user's established preferences. These algorithms utilize user profiles to suggest relevant items, where a user profile typically consists of interaction history, combined with abstract item characteristics and a predictive model such as a decision tree or neural network that infers preferences from past user behavior [35].

1.1.6 Evaluation Measures

As we have seen, there are multiple techniques that can go into an IR system. How do we judge one system over another? In information retrieval tasks, metrics such as precision and recall are commonly used to compare different IR systems.

1.1.6.1 Precision, Recall, and F-Measure

Precision, recall, and F-measure are defined as follows [36, 37]:

1. Precision is the fraction of retrieved documents that are relevant
2. Recall is the fraction of relevant documents that are retrieved.
3. F-measure is the harmonic mean of Precision and Recall.

For example, assume a user has a query q, a set of test collection S, and a set of R relevant documents judged relevant by humans for q. when we run query q against our IR system, we obtain a result set A. We also define $|A|$ as the total number of documents in the result set and $|R|$ as the total number of judged relevant documents. Then we can define our measures as:

1. Precision is the fraction of retrieved documents A that are relevant.

$$Precision = |R \cap A|/|A|$$

2. Recall is the fraction of relevant documents R which have been retrieved.

$$Recall = |R \cap A|/|R|$$

3. F-measure or balanced F-score (F_1) is the harmonic mean of *Precision* and *Recall*.

$$F_1 = \frac{2}{Recall^{-1} + Precision^{-1}}.$$

Many good IR systems aim to maximize precision and recall, but in practice, there is a trade-off between the two. Sometimes users want high precision on the first page of their search results. While in field-specific systems, maximizing recall is a good practice.

1.1.6.2 Precision@k and Recall@k

Many modern search engines provide a ranked list of relevant documents to the user. However, the user cannot explore every relevant document retrieved by the system. *Precision@k* evaluates precision by considering only the top-k documents:

$$P@k = (1/k) * \sum_{n=1}^{k} r_n, \tag{1.5}$$

where r_n is the relevance score of the n-th retrieved document.

Recall@k calculates, of the total relevant documents, the fraction that were retrieved in top-k positions by the IR system:

$$P@k = (1/RB) * \sum_{n=1}^{k} r_n, \tag{1.6}$$

where RB is the total number of relevant documents.

1.1.6.3   Average Precision

Average precision is the average of precision scores at each recall level [38].

$$AP(r) = \sum_{i=1}^{N_q} P_i(r)/N_q, \tag{1.7}$$

where $AP(r)$ is the average precision at recall level r, N_q is the total number of queries used to test the system, and $P_i(r)$ is the precision at level r for the i-th query. Average precision is one of the most common ways to evaluate IR systems, as the behavior of IR systems over the entire test query set can be checked.

1.1.6.4   Discounted Cumulated Gain

DCG deals with the idea that a relevant document appearing lower in search results should be penalized [39]. DCG at rank K is defined as:

$$DCG(k) = \sum_{n=1}^{k} r_n/\max(1, \log_b(n)). \tag{1.8}$$

For a query, Normalized Discounted Cumulated Gain, or NDCG, is computed as:

$$NDCG(k) = DCG(k)/iDCG(k). \tag{1.9}$$

NDCG is the ratio of DCG(k) for a query, by the DCG(k) of the ideal run.

1.2   Bias in Information Retrieval

IR systems are observed to deliver results that can exhibit undesirable or even wrongful forms of bias. Such biases range from perpetuating harmful stereotypes to creating unequal access of opportunity. The following examples highlight reported examples of biased IR systems.

1.2.1   Examples of Documented Biases in IR Systems

The groundbreaking work *Algorithms of Oppression* highlighted the hyper-sexualized results returned by the Google search engine for innocuous search queries like *black girls*, *Asian girls*, and *American Indian girls*. These results were often linked to pornographic content despite the non-sexual nature of the queries, and stood in stark contrast to still biased but non-pornographic results returned for another innocuous query, *white girls*, revealing a pattern of biased results for queries concerning minority groups [12].

The issue of harm to minorities also extends to image search. Search results for the query 'CEO' primarily return male-dominated results [40], reinforcing the stereotype of associating men with leadership roles. Searching for the query *three black teenagers* on Google predominantly returned images of mugshots, while the query *three white teenagers* delivered neutral results [12]. A Google Vision system mislabeled a thermometer as a firearm only when it was held by a dark skinned hand [41]. It recognized the thermometer correctly when held by a hand with a lighter skin color. The biased image tagging by algorithmic systems is dangerous as the law enforcement agencies use the data to identify criminals and if such computer vision systems are blatantly biased, then it harms already marginalized communities. Another concern of such tagging systems is that they are used to label huge datasets, which are then used by machine learning models for downstream applications. If the labels are wrongfully tagged, it can then impact the performance of downstream software applications and again, harm minority communities.

Modern image generation tools such as Stable Diffusion also perpetuate similar biases [42]. When *prompted* to generate images of a person from Australia or North America, the returned results frequently erase Indigenous populations and default to returning images of a Western, light-skinned man.

Another famous example of biases caused by IR systems comes from a hiring platform developed by Amazon. The system trained on the company's past hiring data trained itself to prefer resumes from male candidates [43]. This system learned to downrank resumes that contain words like *women's*, and even to give a lower score to resumes for candidates from all-women colleges. Automated hiring systems are used to narrow down candidates to be interviewed for the role, and a biased system can harm minority groups– in this case, female candidates– by denying them a potential career opportunity.

Similar biases can also happen in the world of online ad-targeting. Platforms are more likely to serve ads for leadership roles to men while showing ads for lower-paying secretarial roles to women. The biased and opaque ecosystem can lead to loss of opportunities for some users, as they will not even be aware of opportunities for which they are qualified. In some cases, Harm can even be more direct, as demonstrated by Latanya Sweeney, who found that searching for names stereotypically associated with Black individuals [44] is significantly more likely to trigger ads for arrest records search services, unjustly associating them with criminality and potentially impacting their personal and professional reputations.

Beyond societal biases, significant harm can also be caused by architectural design and economic incentives of IR systems. Many systems, particularly social media platforms, are designed to maximize user engagement, as longer screen time translates directly to higher ad revenue. Platforms like Instagram and TikTok employ a suite of behavioral techniques from triggers like push notifications to rewards such as *likes* and *replies* to hook users onto the platforms. The constant dopamine-ridden attention-seeking loop can have severe consequences, contributing to increasing rates of depression, lack of attention span, and anxiety among adolescents [45–48].

An engagement-driven model also creates a biased information ecosystem: platforms may decide to amplify certain posts to make them 'go viral' while 'shadowbanning', suppressing the reach of some content and creators without much explanation [49, 50].

1.2.2 Categories of Harms Caused by IR Systems

The examples of bias discussed above can be categorized into three types of harms, as defined by Barocas et al. [10]. It is crucial to understand the different harms caused by the IR systems for identifying and mitigating them effectively.

Consumer Harm. Occurs when systems provide better information to certain *consumers* and discriminate against others. Collaborative filtering-based recommender systems use ratings and feedback from similar users to suggest new content. For users in a minority group that does not provide enough feedback or are not active on the platform, the system doesn't learn enough about the users to suggest relevant content, and provides less relevant suggestions compared to suggestions for users in the majority group. An example of consumer harm comes from an investigation by ProPublica highlighting that the Princeton Review was charging different prices for SAT prep based on zip codes submitted on the company website; higher income areas were offered higher prices regardless of the individual's economic background seeking the prep services [51].

Producer Harm. Occurs when platforms exercise broad power through actions that lack accountability toward the users who provide content. There are reported examples of platforms such as YouTube and other social media platforms suppressing the reach of certain creators, which in turn harms the creators' ability to earn ad revenue. Other incidents of platform bias towards their properties over other producers on the platform, social media partisan bias in promoting certain content over others, also fall under this category [10, 49].

Representational Harm. Arises when choices made by the system perpetuate harmful cultural stereotypes. Gender bias and racial bias have continued to plague Google, as highlighted by results returned for queries like 'black girls' and 'CEO' [12, 40]. A foundational goal for any IR system must be to avoid worsening and amplifying harmful stereotypical biases.

1.2.3 Conclusion

Finally, it is crucial to recognize that many harms in certain IR systems, such as social media recommender systems, are not accidental byproducts of complicated search systems, but are consequences of carefully designed algorithmic models incentivized to generate more user engagement and increase revenue through ad-delivery systems. User engagement is a core metric, as the content that can deliver more clicks often translates to increased ad visibility and more revenue. These economic incentives and the search engine optimization (SEO) tactics used to encourage the search engine to promote certain content can ensure that such material ranks highly for targeted keywords. This creates powerful economic incentives to prioritize content that is sensational, provocative, or enraging, regardless of its quality or societal impact [45–48, 52]. Understanding this economic engine is a prerequisite for diagnosing the root causes of bias, which will be the focus of the next chapter.

In this book, we explore different harms caused by Information Retrieval systems and ways to mitigate such biases through different data and algorithmic interventions.

In Chap. 2, we dive into causes of unfairness in IR systems. We highlight how cultural biases lead to statistical biases, which impact the performance of IR systems. In Chap. 3, we discuss different methods to measure unfairness/bias in search results and word embeddings. We then present high-level algorithmic designs that can be used to mitigate biases. In Chapt. 4, we explain different word embedding methods and present methods that can be used to mitigate biases at the word embedding level and deliver balanced word embeddings. In Chap. 5 provides algorithms to tackle biases in IR and to deliver results that satisfy criteria such as statistical parity and individual-level fairness. Lastly, in Chap. 6, we briefly discuss the potential dangers of using LLMs based IR systems.

References

1. Bush V et al (1945) As we may think. The Atlantic Monthly 176(1):101–108
2. Ricardo A (1999) Baeza-yates and Berthier Ribeiro-Neto, modern information retrieval. Addison-Wesley Longman Publishing Co. Inc, USA
3. Luhn HP (1957) A statistical approach to mechanized encoding and searching of literary information. IBM J Res Dev 1(4):309–317
4. Luhn HP (1953) A new method of recording and searching information. Am Doc 4(1):14–16
5. Manning CD, Raghavan P, Schütze H (2008) Introduction to information retrieval. Cambridge University Press
6. Salton G (1971) The SMART retrieval system-experiments in automatic document processing. Prentice-Hall Inc, USA
7. Salton G, Buckley C (1988) Term-weighting approaches in automatic text retrieval. Inf Proc Manage 24(5):513–523
8. Floridi L, Chiriatti M (2020) Gpt-3: its nature, scope, limits, and consequences. Minds Mach 30(4):681–694
9. Team G, Anil R, Borgeaud S, Alayrac J-B, Yu J, Soricut R, Schalkwyk J, Dai AM, Hauth A, Millican K et al (2025) Gemini: a family of highly capable multimodal models
10. Barocas S, Hardt M, Narayanan A (2023) Fairness and machine learning: limitations and opportunities. MIT Press
11. Chen J, Dong H, Wang X, Feng F, Wang M, He X (2023) Bias and debias in recommender system: a survey and future directions. ACM Trans Inf Syst 41(3)
12. Noble SU (2018) Algorithms of oppression: how search engines reinforce racism. NYU Press
13. Wang Y, Ma W, Zhang M, Liu Y, Ma S (2023) A survey on the fairness of recommender systems. ACM Trans Inf Syst 41(3)

14. Sanderson M, Bruce Croft W (2012) The history of information retrieval research. Proceedings of the IEEE 100(Special Centennial Issue):1444–1451

15. Salton G, Lesk ME (1968) Computer evaluation of indexing and text processing. J ACM 15(1):8–36

16. Bollmann-Sdorra P, Raghavan VV (1993) On the delusiveness of adopting a common space for modeling ir objects: are queries documents? J Am Soc Inf Sci 44(10):579–587

17. Wong SKM, Ziarko W, Raghavan VV, Wong PCN (1987) On modeling of information retrieval concepts in vector spaces. ACM Trans Database Syst 12(2):299–321

18. Kobayashi M, Takeda K (2000) Information retrieval on the web. ACM Comput Surv 32(2):144–173

19. Schatz BR (1997) Information retrieval in digital libraries: bringing search to the net. Science 275(5298):327–334

20. Lawrence S, Lee Giles C (2000) Accessibility of information on the web. Intelligence 11(1):32–39

21. Nielsen J (1995) Multimedia and hypertext: the internet and beyond. Academic Press Professional Inc, USA

22. Shneiderman B, Kearsley G (1989) Hypertext hands-on-an introduction to a new way of organizing and accessing information. Addison-Wesley Longman Publishing Co. Inc, USA

23. Henzinger M (2000) Link analysis in web information retrieval. IEEE Data (Base) Eng Bull 23:3–8

24. Brin S, Page L (1998) The anatomy of a large-scale hypertextual web search engine. Comput Netw ISDN Syst 30(1):107–117. Proceedings of the seventh international world wide web conference

25. Henzinger M (2000) Web information retrieval–an algorithmic perspective. In: Paterson MS (ed) Algorithms–ESA 2000 Berlin, Heidelberg. Springer, Berlin Heidelberg, pp 1–8

26. Page L, Brin S, Motwani R, Winograd T (1998) The PageRank citation ranking: bringing order to the web. Technical report, Stanford Digital Library Technologies Project

27. Bharat K, Broder A (1998) A technique for measuring the relative size and overlap of public web search engines. Comput Netw ISDN Syst 30(1):379–388. Proceedings of the Seventh International World Wide Web Conference

28. Lawrence S, Lee Giles C (1998) Searching the world wide web. Science 280(5360):98–100

29. Cho J, Garcia-Molina H (2000) The evolution of the web and implications for an incremental crawler. In: Proceedings of the 26th international conference on very large data bases, VLDB '00, page 200–209, San Francisco, CA, USA. Morgan Kaufmann Publishers Inc

30. Coffman EG Jr, Liu Z, Weber RR (1998) Optimal robot scheduling for Web search engines. J Schedul 1(1):15–29

31. Bharat K, Broder A, Henzinger M, Kumar P, Venkatasubramanian S (1998) The connectivity server: fast access to linkage information on the web. Comput. Netw ISDN Syst 30(1):469–477 (1998). Proceedings of the seventh international world wide web conference

32. Dean J, Henzinger MR (1999) Finding related pages in the world wide web. Comput Netw 31(11–16):1467–1479

33. Anick PG, Vaithyanathan S (1997) Exploiting clustering and phrases for context-based information retrieval. In: Proceedings of the 20th annual international ACM SIGIR conference on research and development in information retrieval, pp 314–323

34. He Q (1999) A review of clustering algorithms as applied in ir. Grad Sch Libr Inf Sci Univ Ill Urbana-Champaign 6:1–33

35. Aggarwal CC (2016) Recommender systems: the textbook, 1st edn. Springer Publishing Company, Incorporated

36. Van Rijsbergen CJ (1974) Foundation of evaluation. J Document 30(4):365–373

37. VAN Rijsbergen CJ (1981) Retrieval effectiveness. Inf Retr Exp 32–43,

38. Buckley C, Voorhees E (2005) Retrieval system evaluation. TREC Chapter to be published: TREC: experiment and evaluation in information retrieval, 2005-09-26 00:09:00 2005

39. Järvelin K, Kekäläinen J (2002) Cumulated gain-based evaluation of ir techniques. ACM Trans Inf Syst 20(4):422–446

40. Feng Y, Shah C (2022) Has CEO gender bias really been fixed? Adversarial attacking and improving gender fairness in image search. In: Proc AAAI Conf Artif Intell 36(11):11882–11890

41. Kayser-Bril N (2025) Google apologizes after its Vision AI produced racist results—AlgorithmWatch—algorithmwatch.org. https://algorithmwatch.org/en/google-vision-racism/. [Accessed 05 Nov 2025]

42. Ghosh S, Caliskan A (2023) 'Person' == Light-skinned, Western Man, and sexualization of women of color: stereotypes in stable diffusion. In: Bouamor H, Pino J, Bali K (eds) Findings of the association for computational linguistics: EMNLP 2023, Singapore. Association for Computational Linguistics, pp 6971–6985

43. Dastin J (2025) Insight—Amazon scraps secret AI recruiting tool that showed bias against women. https://www.reuters.com/article/world/insight-amazon-scraps-secret-ai-recruiting-tool-that-showed-bias-against-women-idUSKCN1MK0AG. [Accessed 05 Nov 2025]

44. Sweeney L (2013) Discrimination in online ad delivery. Commun ACM 56(5):44–54

45. Bulut D (2023) The association between attention impairments and the internet and social media usage among adolescents and young adults with potential consequences: a review of literature. Psychology 14(8):1310–1321

46. Haidt J (2024) The anxious generation: how the great rewiring of childhood is causing an epidemic of mental illness. Penguin Press

47. Hilty DM, Stubbe D, McKean AJ, Hoffman PE, Zalpuri I, Myint MT, Joshi SV, Pakyurek M, Su-Ting TL (2023) A scoping review of social media in child, adolescents and young adults: research findings in depression, anxiety and other clinical challenges. BJPsych Open 9(5):e152

48. Seabrook EM, Kern ML, Rickard NS (2016) Social networking sites, depression, and anxiety: a systematic review. JMIR Mental Health 3(4)

49. Duffy BE, Meisner C (2023) Platform governance at the margins: social media creators' experiences with algorithmic (in)visibility. Med Cult Soc 45(2):285–304

50. Horwitz J (2025) Facebook says its rules apply to all. Company Documents Reveal a Secret Elite That's Exempt. https://www.wsj.com/tech/facebook-files-xcheck-zuckerberg-elite-rules-11631541353. [Accessed 05 Nov 2025]

51. Mattu S, Angwin J, Larson J (2025) The tiger mom tax: Asians are nearly twice as likely to get a higher price from princeton review—propublica.org. https://www.propublica.org/article/asians-nearly-twice-as-likely-to-get-higher-price-from-princeton-review. [Accessed 05 Nov 2025]

52. Rhodes SC (2022) Filter bubbles, echo chambers, and fake news: how social media conditions individuals to be less critical of political misinformation. Polit Commun 39(1):1–22

Chapter 2
Unfairness in Information Retrieval

Abstract Recent years have brought a great deal of attention to the existence of unfairness in computational systems, including information retrieval systems. In this chapter, we discuss several causes of unfairness: design choices, selection of target variable, data bias, feature selection, proxy variables, and feedback loop. We then explore each of these causes in depth, providing examples and discussion.

2.1 Overview

IR systems operate within complex socio-technical environments, and multiple factors can introduce unfairness. Unlike unfairness caused by a flawed algorithm or a biased dataset, unfairness in IR systems often emerges from a complex interplay between data, algorithms, and the broader social context in which these systems are deployed.

Relationship between bias and unfairness. In this book, we use 'bias' in the colloquial, rather than the statistical, sense to refer to an unjust prejudice against individuals, commonly based on demographic factors like race or gender. This is how the term is commonly used in the algorithmic fairness literature. In the context of algorithms, bias is the underlying reason an algorithm learns to be partial, favoring one group or individual over another. Conversely, fairness is a guarantee of parity in how all groups or individuals are treated [1]. We define unfairness as the state where this guarantee of fairness is violated.

Bias in data or models may result in various fairness-related issues, and mitigating such biases can help make systems less unfair. Biases exist at different stages in information retrieval systems, such as data, model, and the outcomes [2]. If the data collection process or the sampling process is itself biased then it will cause the model to learn preferences related to over-representative groups better than other groups. Similarly, a model can infer sensitive information from the available data and use them for decision making processes even when the sensitive attributes were explicitly removed from the training process [3, 4].

For example, a model may find a pattern between preferred candidates on the platform and their educational background information. If members of a protected class

© The Author(s), under exclusive license to Springer Nature Switzerland AG 2026   17
H. Mishra and S. Soundarajan, *Addressing Bias in Information Retrieval*,
SpringerBriefs in Intelligent Systems, https://doi.org/10.1007/978-3-032-24145-0_2

have preferred certain group of colleges due to reasons such as tradition, historical prejudices, or redlining, then a model may learn user's protected characteristics, such as race or gender, based on available educational information, even when explicit protected attributes were removed from the collected data. To provide better results, the model may start to favor or disfavor certain candidates based on learned protected characteristics.

Unmitigated bias in these systems may increase process unfairness and outcome unfairness [5]. Process fairness refers to the IR model being fair, such that protected characteristics should not influence either the representation of the data or the learning of the model itself. Outcome fairness in IR systems treats fair outcomes in terms of fair allocation. The outcome is fair if similar individuals are treated similarly or if the groups are treated similarly to their proportion in the demographic.

A majority of existing research in mitigating biases in IR systems focuses on outcome fairness concepts such as individual fairness, group fairness and fair allocation at either the individual or group level. We focus on a discussion related to different outcome fairness categories in the book and refer the readers to [1, 2, 5] for more exhaustive literature on different categorization of fairness concepts.

Understanding the root causes of unfairness is essential for developing fairer IR systems. Only by understanding where and why the bias enters the algorithmic pipeline can we design bias measurement methods and mitigation algorithms. Barocas and Selbst discussed different reasons for how algorithms and data processes can produce discrimination [4]. Although that work was not focused on IR systems, many of their concerns are valid for our use-case as well. We highlight six primary causes of unfairness in IR systems.

1. **Socio-technical Design Choices** can embed unfairness into the design of the system [6].
2. **Target Variable** unfairness arises from how the system defines and optimizes its objective [4].
3. **Data Bias** reflects historical inequities and cultural biases that impact the data collection, training data, and sampling process used in data modeling [4].
4. **Feature Selection** process of choosing which features to include may inadvertently encode or exacerbate disparities. [4]
5. **Proxy Variables** can encode biases in correlated attributes [4].
6. **Feedback Loops** amplify existing biases over time, leading to increasingly unfair systems [3].

These causes can influence each other, creating unfairness that goes beyond one technical component of the system. For example, historic biases in the dataset may reflect in the results of the IR system, which can get amplified due to users' actions. Even if one finds and explicitly removes the protected attributes in the dataset that are the cause of unfairness, due to the presence of proxy variables, the system may still not improve.

After this chapter's discussion on foundational causes of unfairness, Chap. 3 will present multiple ways to measure bias in the word embeddings and ranked output of the IR systems. Providing methods to quantify bias is needed to develop bias mitigation algorithms in subsequent chapters.

We begin our discussion by explaining how the design choices of the IR systems ignore the broader social context environment in which they are deployed, which can induce unfairness in the system even when the developers of the system have *fair* intentions.

2.1.1 Design of Information Retrieval Systems

IR systems do not exist in isolation. They are designed by multiple teams that have specific technical training and also inevitably carry assumptions about the users and use cases of what they build. The design choices, sometimes due to ill intentions but more often stemming from the scale of modern IR systems, result in the models preferring some groups while disadvantaging others. Understanding how design choices create unfairness is crucial to reasoning about the sources of bias that we discuss later in the chapter.

2.1.1.1 Design Choices and Technical Bias

Forsythe et al. studying researchers developing expert systems in the field of medical informatics, noticed a divide between researchers and the users of the systems. She documented the lack of communication between researchers and the end users (albeit for a different problem: that of *user acceptance*). She noticed the culture of teams developing the AI systems and points out *technical bias*: when the focus is on the technical part of the problem, the eagerness to jump to mathematical objectives often ignores non-technical factors, such as whether these systems developed in a way that users will use [7].

In IR systems, such technical bias can manifest with teams highly focused on maximizing a metric such as *relevance* on a test set, without considering fairness-related factors, such as whether the scores are similar across different groups [8]. A search system may deliver high *accuracy* and *relevance* scores overall, but still perform poorly for queries related to minority groups.

Decontextualized thinking. The social context in which humans exist is complex, but due to the abstraction-focused approach that makes up much of the literature in computer science, researchers do away with complexity and focus on simplifying the problem statement until it can fit within a mathematical framework that they have mastered over the years. Often, the evaluation of these methods happens in isolation (research labs) and not with real users in the loop.

2.1.1.2   The Socio-Technical Systems Framework

Recently, Selbst et al. proposed viewing hybrid systems that consists of technical and social components as *sociotechnical systems*, combining technical components as well as social context in which the systems persist [6]. They proposed five abstraction traps resulting from the gap between technical systems and the social world, and a sociotechnical system (STS) lens to deal with different traps:

1. The Framing Trap: The process of just focusing on training data, algorithm's outputs for the input data and to evaluate the algorithm on the training data and its generalizability on the unseen data from similar distribution. The data representation and generated outcomes create an *algorithmic frame.* The goal of the algorithmic frame is to create a model that accurately predict the relationship between the input data and its corresponding output labels. The STS framework calls for moving beyond the algorithmic frame to interrogate assumptions embedded in data collection and labeling, where social values are often baked in. In the *data frame*, social context is brought into the frame by questioning the source of the data and also investigating whether the output labels are defined correctly for the task.
   In IR, this might mean connecting *relevance* with click-through data without investigating whether past biases are reflected in user behavior. A hiring platform can continue to promote candidates from the majority groups while harming those from minorities based on past discriminatory hiring practices [9]. A social media platform might equate user engagement with content relevance. Optimizing for this framing can lead to harmful content being promoted to adolescents, since such content may drive higher engagement. This ignores the broader social consequences, such as negative impacts on mental health [10].
   Algorithms are often evaluated on benchmark datasets before they are deployed for public use. The benchmark datasets may have a data bias with respect to under-representation of certain communities. Therefore, even when the model is optimized and perfected on available datasets, they will still be harmful when used by general public consisting of diverse groups [11, 12].
2. The Portability Trap: The idea that good code should be portable is deeply ingrained in trained computer scientists and engineers. This leads to a portability problem for machine learning models: a fairness definition is fixed, an evaluation framework is selected, and the model is then ported to different applications. Guided only by broad tasks such as classification, clustering, regression, etc., designers may ignore the context of the application, which can range from recidivism and loan defaults to customer churning, to name a few [13, 14]. A recommendation algorithm designed to keep users longer on the platform may work for an e-commerce platform, but if a similar strategy is used for news-based social media, then it can lead to increased polarization and amplification of extreme content [15, 16].
3. The Formalism Trap: Algorithms speak in math, while concepts such as fairness often rely on procedural terms. It is easy to consider a fairness task, select a fairness

definition, and implement lines of code to deliver the required solution, ignoring that fairness in a social context is *contestable*: decisions can be contested in public spaces and the definitions of fairness can evolve with ever-changing social norms. A static piece of code codifying fairness does not change with the evolving norms of the society. Fairness in a non-abstract environment depends on the context in which a decision was made, as well as procedural fairness, which takes time to judge a decision, unlike fair-ML algorithms, where outcomes are zero-shot decisions without any space to argue against the algorithmic decision [6].

IR systems often use a rigid mathematical definition of fairness, whereas societies change with an evolving understanding of fairness. An IR system should adapt to changing social norms [17–19].

4. The Ripple Effect Trap: Technology can have unintended consequences on people in which the systems are placed. We need to study how the system and users interact with each other, along with scores reported on the evaluation metrics, to truly understand if the proposed ML system is fair or not.

   For example, even if a recommender system is initially deployed with the understanding that the data is imbalanced (and with corresponding mechanisms to mitigate bias), over time, that nuance may be forgotten, and the system used at face value harms groups that are in the minority in the dataset [20].

5. The Solutionism Trap: Not every real-world problem can be codified using math and programming languages. This occurs commonly in an areas where social constructs rapidly evolve, or the law changes over time. Using computer models will only work if they are not set in stone: that is, if they are iterative, change with time, or at least take into account the evolving value judgments of society.

   Some problems plaguing society may not have a technical solution rooted in IR. For example, problems like loneliness may best be resolved with increased public discourse rather than by an AI friend IR platform [21, 22].

   The AI chat-bots that are developed specifically for mental healthcare such as Moodfit and Therachat, or even general chat-bots such as ChatGPT, can provide access to personalized support at finger tips but they also bring along ethical issues that are yet to be resolved. They are not medical professionals trained for care, guidance and non verbal cues to understand mental state of their patient. Even the most advanced chat-bots currently, may return inaccurate or harmful advice which can prove detrimental to an individual's mental health [22, 23].

These design-level choices impact the data, algorithmic, and feedback-based causes of unfairness that we discuss in subsequent sections. For example, the technical bias discussed above can lead to flawed data mining practices (Sect. 2.3.2). Recognizing socio-technical traps is essential to anticipate different causes of unfairness that can impact an IR system.

2.2 Target Variables

Machine learning models are trained using an objective function that incorporates target labels. During training, the model learns to minimize error rates and perform well on the evaluation set. Defining the target variable is crucial for solving the problem at hand, as selecting an incorrect target variable can lead the model to optimize for a different problem than the one we intend to solve [4].

For example, consider a social media platform. If its target variable is user engagement, the system may learn to promote extreme sensational content that can generate more clicks and shares. Alternatively, if the platform instead defines its target variable as user well-being, it might optimize for signals such as sustained positive interactions, reduced exposure to harmful content, or long-term satisfaction.[1] Similarly, a hiring platform might define its target variable as employee retention. In that case, it could optimize for candidates with a history of longer tenures, even though it may disadvantage candidates with short employment cycles.

Selection of a target variable is inherently subjective and part of the design choice for the system. Once deployed, these choices shape the behavior of the system and its downstream social impact.

2.3 Data Bias

Modern search engines require vast amounts of data to deliver results that are relevant, personalized, and economically valuable. Web crawlers continually traverse the internet, indexing a large portion of accessible content. The entire process, from submitting the query to a search engine to obtaining a list of results, demands a vast quantity of data to find relevant content for the user's query. The scale of data collection makes it infeasible to manually audit each and every item for harmful, possibly discriminatory content. As a result, the historic and current cultural prejudices embedded in data and used by the IR systems inevitably shape the IR systems to deliver biased results. In the following subsections, we explain how culture influences the data pipeline and, in turn, affects the output of IR systems.

2.3.1 Historical Bias

As discussed in Chap. 1, the sexualization of minority women depicted in media often finds its way to search engine results [24, 25].

For example, the hyper-sexualized query auto-complete suggestions and search results for queries like *black girls* and *Asian girls* are opposite to results retrieved for queries such as *white girls*. Multiple other examples show that the results were

---

[1] The system may decide to log out the user entirely from the platform to prioritize user happiness.

far more harmful when queries related to minority groups were used compared to queries dealing with groups in the majority. This is not an isolated incident but a reflection of centuries of racial prejudices that have found their way into mainstream content in the form of news, books, magazine articles, radio, TV shows, movies, and now websites [26, 27]. The widespread digitization in the latter part of the last century led to a vast transfer of knowledge onto the internet, including documented discriminatory practices of the past [25, 28, 29].

Data bias plays a crucial role in understanding why a search engine delivers harmful results when searching for a type of query, such as delivering higher-quality results when dealing with queries about non-marginalized groups. Suppose certain groups have historically been harmfully marginalized in widely consumed content. In that case, it is quite likely that even an algorithmically unaware, unbiased search engine will also return discriminatory results for queries related to those groups [28, 30, 31]. Search engine results can not only reflect the biases present in the dataset, but they can also perpetuate and amplify such biases (Sect. 2.6).

An example of data *data bias* occurs when we query terms such as *Doctor* and *Nurse* to the search engine: for the query *Doctor*, the algorithm has slightly more data about male doctors than female doctors, but the search results exaggerate this effect to return disproportionately more results about male doctors than female doctors [32–34]. This is an example of stereotype exaggeration, where image results exhibit a slight exaggeration based on stereotypical attitudes which can continue to reinforce biases and potentially influence people's perception of gender distribution in certain occupations [32].

Search engine algorithms, when looking for content most relevant to the user query (which might even be a query modified at the backend, perhaps by adding tail keywords), may return harmful results to the end user. *Algorithmic bias* exacerbates the issue: for example, ranking algorithms are often designed to prioritize content they predict will be most relevant and engaging, with historical click-through rates serving as a significant signal in this prediction [35, 36]. Suppose the end user, out of curiosity, or with malicious intentions, or misled by snippets, clicks on the content; the click is treated as a signal to the algorithm that the user engaged with the content. The algorithm then boosts the visibility of such content for other users. It is known that such boosted content can influence people in some demographic groups, and the opacity of algorithmic bias also makes sure that the end users are not aware of any algorithmic effect changing their attitudes or beliefs [37].[2]

Loneliness and social exclusion have been linked to the process of radicalization [38]. Recent studies further highlight that sustained use of social media and prolonged exposure to negative content often facilitated/ amplified by recommendation systems and personalized search can exacerbate mental health issues. When factors such as loneliness, psychological distress, and offline effects like isolation

---

[2] Another important issue is of *lack of diversity* in teams that develop such systems. If the search engine team had people from diverse backgrounds, then it is possible someone would have searched for the simple queries discussed above, and caught the issue before it made its way into Noble's book *Algorithms of Oppression* [25].

are combined with behavior such as 'doom scrolling' or engagement in fringe topics promoted by algorithms, they can provide a pathway towards radicalization and in some cases, harmful real-world outcomes [16, 39–41].

2.3.2 Imbalanced Data

IR systems rely on algorithms and a dataset to return a set of relevant results to the user. The behavior of a system is greatly dependent on the dataset that is being used. If the collected data contains any prior biases, then the same will be reflected (and possibly amplified) by the outputs of the IR system. In 2016, it was reported that when 'stephanie williams' was searched on LinkedIn, the site automatically *corrected* it to 'stephan williams' [42]. When the same search was repeated with other female first names, paired with placeholder last names, LinkedIn continued to suggest that they change the names, from *Andrea Jones* to *Andrew Jones*, and *Alexa* to *Alex*. When the platform was searched for stereotypically-male names, no such suggestion appeared.

While the exact cause of these examples is unknown, a possible explanation for this phenomenon is that the platform was used for a lot more searches of male contacts, and the platform had a much larger presence of males than females during the time of the incident. Because of this, the search engine, in its duty to deliver the most relevant content to the end user, frequently triggered the auto-correct feature, 'correcting' *Alex* to *Alexa*. A spokeswoman for LinkedIn told BBC that 'Suggestions of similar spelt names that are frequently searched for on LinkedIn will follow the search query, The search algorithm is guided by relative frequencies of words appearing in past queries and member profiles, it is not anything to do [with] gender' [43].

The process of data collection is crucial for modern machine learning systems as results, if derived from biased data, such as data that under-represents protected classes, or non-representative data that is not proportionate to the real world, may return discriminatory results to the users. The quality of data collection can be impacted by various factors, such as ease of abstraction (use of average data for a zip code based on government reports instead of door-to-door surveys), past prejudices (exclusion of data that relates to minority communities), and lack of awareness of past harmful practices such as redlining[3] [4, 44]. Biased data mining practices can make an IR system produce biased results. A hiring platform for a company that traditionally only hired male candidates will have a lot more data about successful male candidates. When the platform is deployed in practice, it will seek to find resumes similar to those in its dataset marked as successful. Due to biased hiring practices of the past, it will rank the female resumes lower than male candidates.

Information Retrieval (IR) models learn patterns from training datasets and return ranked results or a set of results for the user. When training data contains disproportionate representation across different labels or categories, with some heavily

---

[3] Redlining is a discriminatory practice that results in systematic denial of services to certain areas based on race or ethnicity.

overrepresented while others are marginal in quantity, the models then develop systematic biases in favor of the majority classes [45]. This imbalance creates a critical deployment concern: models may achieve strong performance on overrepresented categories due to abundant training examples while simultaneously under-performing on minority classes. Such disparities often remain hidden during evaluation because standard metrics like accuracy and relevance scores appear satisfactory when test sets mirror the same imbalanced distributions present in training data [8].

2.3.3 Encoding Stereotypes Into Word Vectors

In this section, we discuss an example of data bias that emerges in the early stages of model training: word embeddings. When biases present in training data are encoded into vector representations, they propagate through the entire algorithmic pipeline, making the overall system biased.

In a word embedding, text data is converted into numerical vectors, which can then be given as input to various machine learning algorithms, such as those used in web search, spam classification, sentiment analysis, document parsing, etc. Embedding algorithms use surrounding words to learn a meaningful representation of the target word. If the context around the word is biased in a harmful manner, then the embeddings derived from the data may also contain the biases. We discuss word embeddings and ways to debias them in Chap. 4. Here, we describe reasons why word embeddings can contain harmful biases.

The implicit association test proposed by Greenwald et al. [46] highlights significant unconscious biases associated with words. In this association task, the end user needs to associate a word with one of two categories. In general, end users associate words such as *flowers* with the category *pleasant*, and words such as *insects* with the category *unpleasant*. Researchers observed that European American-sounding names were more significantly associated with the *pleasant* category as compared to a stereotypically African-American names. This finding also concurs with the famous study by Bertrand and Mullainathan [47], in which researchers sent 5000 resumes to 1300 job postings; their findings highlighted that the European American-sounding names were more likely to receive an interview than candidates with non-European American names. Such explicit and implicit biases are part of the real-world fabric, and these cultural stereotypes and implicit associations then find their way into text corpora [48, 49]. This harmfully biased text data is then used as input to find a vector representation for words through the word embedding models.

Seminal work by Bolukbasi et al. showcased the sexism issue present in word embeddings [50]. An analogy is used to describe pair of words, where the relationship between the words in each pair is same, and the word embeddings generated biased analogies such as *midwife:doctor*, *giggle:chuckle*, *feminism:conservatism*, *nude:shirtless*, and *nurse:surgeon*. Interestingly, a study on the w2vNEWS embedding generated from a Google News dataset and replicated the similar biased analogies on embedding generated from the GloVe model [51]. The issues of sexism in Google News embeddings were surprising at first glance, as the corpus mostly contains news related data from professional journalists.

Analogy-related tasks are useful tests to showcase real-world relationships extracted through text data, as well as for judging the quality of the embeddings. An analogy task can be used to represent relationships such as *France:Paris::Japan:x*. Using basic vector arithmetic and word embeddings, we can solve the problem as $x = Tokyo$. But the same word embeddings can also 'solve' the problem of *man:computer programmer::woman:x* with $x = homemaker$. The implicit sexism present in off-the-shelf word embeddings makes tools like document ranking, resume parsing, and sentiment analysis harmful for wider public use.

The widespread gender bias prevalent in journalism has long been documented in the Gender Studies literature [26, 52]. Therefore, harmful biases in any word embedding model derived from news data should be considered an expected outcome, rather than an exception.

Similar to the IAT test [46], Bolukbasi et al. [50], and Caliskan et al. [53] developed tests to show the presence of sexism in word embeddings. The tests highlighted how terms like *arts* and *family* were closer to female terms such as *she, woman*, and *girl* than to male terms such as *he, man*, and *boy*, while terms such as *builder* and *genius* were closer to male terms than female terms. More sexualized words were observed to be closer to terms associated with the female gender compared to terms associated with the male gender.

Word embeddings excel at learning semantic relationships between frequent words. Suppose, if a group uses language differently as compared to those in the majority, then the embeddings will not have a significant understanding of the terms. In this scenario, the tools such as hiring platforms, question-answering chat-bots, web based IR systems, will not be able to recommend quality documents related to minorities with same frequency as documents from the majority groups.

2.4 Feature Selection

Feature selection is the process of choosing attributes and related data used by machine learning models. Design decisions at this stage can have serious implications, as marginalized groups may be harmed when selected features fail to represent their characteristics with sufficient granularity. For example, a hiring platform might choose to use the reputation of a candidate's college or university as an attribute instead of their GPA. This approach can disadvantage members of marginalized groups that have historically been underrepresented at prestigious institutions. Even when employers intend to evaluate candidates holistically, biased outputs from systems with poorly designed feature selection processes can influence hiring committee decisions [6].

2.5 Proxy Variables: Redundant Encoding of Bias

Information Retrieval (IR) systems often attempt to mitigate discrimination by excluding protected attributes such as race, gender, or sexual orientation from their data. While this may appear to remove bias, in practice, it is often ineffective because the dataset also contains proxy variables: features that are highly correlated with the sensitive (protected) attributes. Redundant encoding of the bias still makes the system deliver similar biased results even after explicit protected attributes have been removed from the system [4].

We can trace the close correlation between protected attributes and proxy variables by examining historic inequalities and the modern web, which is built to mine users' data as much as it is built for users. For example, consider historic *redlining*, where neighborhoods were racially segregated, versus its current form, where services such as banking, education and healthcare availability can impact the type of populations that live in an area [4, 44]. Even an IR system that excludes explicit race attributes may still deliver biased results due to the presence of proxy attributes such as zipcode, income, and educational background. Similarly, an IR system may decide to exclude gender, but due to modern data collection processes, the system can still learn similar patterns through proxies such as browsing habits, e-commerce activity, and data collected from social media [54].

Recommendation systems such as those on YouTube, Instagram, and TikTok prefer to recommend content that will lead to screen time and generate more engagement. Higher screen-time and engagement lead to more chances to deliver advertisements and collect more user data for more precise targeted advertising, which in turn leads to increased revenue. If historical engagement by a user contains racial, gender, or politically biased content, then in the name of delivering personalized results, the system learns to promote content that reflects prior prejudices captured by the IR system.

Even when specific data is not explicitly collected, data available for free on the web, such as engagement behavior on social media (likes, replies, friend-follow graph) can make algorithms powerful enough to detect personnel information such as sexual preference, race, political alignment of a user [4, 54].

2.6 Feedback Loops and Algorithmic Amplification of Bias

IR systems observe and store user engagement data in order to deliver relevant and personalized results to the user. Such results may include click-through rates, time spent on a product page on an e-commerce platform, or the most frequent items that lead to user engagement. This process blends personal data observed for a user with data collected from other users. In a feedback loop, a user engages with an item, the algorithm updates itself with user preferences, and then returns results that satisfy the captured user preferences [35, 55].

If the user has shown prior biases in their engagement with the platform, then the biases may reflect in subsequent results. Over time, the algorithm starts to show more extreme content to increase user engagement, which can be quantified in terms of likes, replies, and time spent on the platform. The move from reflecting existing biases to promoting extreme content to drive more engagement leads to amplification of bias driven by IR algorithms [55–57].

For example, a platform such as YouTube or Facebook can learn a user's political preferences based on the user's behavior on their platform, and over time, begins to promote content with more extreme political views, which makes the engaged user spend more time engaging with the content on the platform. This leads to increased polarization in society, where users with different political beliefs are put in isolated 'filter bubbles.' In these filter bubbles, systems continue to reinforce and amplify existing beliefs, which can lead to real-world harms.

An example of this occurred when Facebook became one of the primary news sources in Myanmar. In the 2010s, Myanmar military personnel began to use Facebook to spread hate against Myanmar's Muslim population. These government personnel created Facebook pages devoted to Myanmar celebrities, and once the pages garnered large followings, officials began distributing unfounded claims, false news, and inflammatory posts aimed at the Myanmar's Muslim population. The explosive growth of social media in Myanmar was partly due to Facebook itself, with people spending much more of their time online, following content that they 'like', combined with troll accounts posting fake inflammatory posts, showed how unmoderated filter bubbles can have disastrous consequences. Because platforms such as Facebook rely on engagement based metrics, one of their aim is to keep users on the platform for as long as possible, and inflammatory content accomplished this goal, leading to such posts becoming viral on the platform. The violent fake content and Facebook's engagement methods created an echo chamber which ultimately led to real world harms. The heightened tensions resulted in real world consequences, including murders and rapes, using a digital platform as a tool for ethnic cleansing [58–62].

Similar examples of increased amplification of biased results have been reported in adolescents on social media platforms. Platforms such as Instagram, TikTok recommend negative content to the users, such as unhealthy bodily standards pushed through content recommended to teenage boys and girls. Amplified harmful content along with behavioral tricks such as external triggers in form of frequent notifications, variable reward presented in form of likes or replies the user may or may not have received, internal triggers where the users gets used to dopamine hits by opening the platforms and staying on them for long durations. Behavioral tricks such as push notifications or variable rewards used by the platforms to keep the users scrolling and consuming the harmful content may lead to cases of depression in young adults [10, 63–65].

Understanding the feedback loops and the role of IR systems in amplification of harmful content is necessary in order to actively mitigate harmful real-world harms caused by the IR systems.

References

1. Chouldechova A, Roth A (2020) A snapshot of the frontiers of fairness in machine learning. Commun ACM 63(5):82–89
2. Chen J, Dong H, Wang X, Feng F, Wang M, He X (2023) Bias and debias in recommender system: a survey and future directions. ACM Trans Inf Syst 41(3)
3. Barocas S, Hardt M, Narayanan A (2023) Fairness and machine learning: Limitations and opportunities. MIT Press
4. Barocas S, Selbst AD (2016) Big data's disparate impact. Calif Law Rev 104(3):671–732
5. Wang Y, Ma W, Zhang M, Liu Y, Ma S (2023) A survey on the fairness of recommender systems. ACM Trans Inf Syst 41(3)
6. Selbst AD, Boyd D, Friedler SA, Venkatasubramanian S, Vertesi J (2019) Fairness and abstraction in sociotechnical systems. In: Proceedings of the conference on fairness, accountability, and transparency, New York, NY, USA, pp 59–68. ACM
7. Forsythe D, Hess DJ (2001) Studying those who study us: an anthropologist in the world of artificial intelligence. Stanford University Press, Stanford, Calif, Writing science
8. Amini A, Soleimany AP, Schwarting W, Bhatia SN, Rus D (2019) Uncovering and mitigating algorithmic bias through learned latent structure. In: Proceedings of the 2019 AAAI/ACM conference on AI, ethics, and society, AIES '19, pp 289–295, New York, NY, USA. Association for Computing Machinery
9. Dastin J (2022) Amazon scraps secret AI recruiting tool that showed bias against women. In: Ethics of data and analytics, vol 1. CRC Press, 1 edition, pp 296–299
10. Hilty DM, Stubbe D, McKean AJ, Hoffman PE, Zalpuri I, Myint MT, Joshi SV, Pakyurek M, Li S-TT (2023) A scoping review of social media in child, adolescents and young adults: research findings in depression, anxiety and other clinical challenges. BJPsych Open 9(5):e152-2023
11. Schwemmer C, Knight C, Bello-Pardo ED, Oklobdzija S, Schoonvelde M, Lockhart JW (2020) Diagnosing gender bias in image recognition systems. Media Cult Soc 6:1–17
12. Yang K, Qinami K, Fei-Fei L, Deng J, Russakovsky O (2020) Towards fairer datasets: filtering and balancing the distribution of the people subtree in the ImageNet hierarchy. In: Proceedings of the 2020 conference on fairness, accountability, and transparency, FAT* '20, New York, NY, USA, pp 547–558. Association for Computing Machinery
13. Kamishima T, Akaho S, Asoh H, Sakuma J, Flach PA, De Bie T, Cristianini N (2012) Fairness-aware classifier with prejudice remover regularizer. Machine Learning and Knowledge Discovery in Databases. volume 7524 of Lecture Notes in Computer Science. Springer, Berlin Heidelberg, Berlin, Heidelberg, pp 35–50
14. Zafar MB, Valera I, Gomez Rodriguez M, Gummadi KP (2017) Fairness beyond disparate treatment and disparate impact: learning classification without disparate mistreatment. In: Proceedings of the 26th international conference on world wide web, WWW '17, pp 1171–1180, Republic and Canton of Geneva, CHE, 2017. International world wide web conferences steering committee
15. Lim SL, Bentley PJ (2022) Opinion amplification causes extreme polarization in social networks. Sci Rep 12(1):18131
16. Roose K (2019) The making of a YouTube radical (Published 2019)—nytimes.com. https://www.nytimes.com/interactive/2019/06/08/technology/youtube-radical.html. [Accessed 06 Nov 2025]
17. Chouldechova A (2017) Fair prediction with disparate impact: a study of bias in recidivism prediction instruments. Big data 5(2):153–163
18. Feldman M, Friedler SA, Moeller J, Scheidegger C, Venkatasubramanian S (2015) Certifying and removing disparate impact. In: Proceedings of the 21th ACM SIGKDD international conference on knowledge discovery and data mining, KDD '15, New York, NY, USA, pp 259–268. Association for Computing Machinery
19. Grgić-Hlača N, Zafar MB, Gummadi KP, Weller A (2018) Beyond distributive fairness in algorithmic decision making: feature selection for procedurally fair learning. In: Proceedings of the

thirty-second AAAI conference on artificial intelligence and thirtieth innovative applications of artificial intelligence conference and eighth AAAI symposium on educational advances in artificial intelligence, AAAI'18/IAAI'18/EAAI'18. AAAI Press

20. Stevenson M (2018) Assessing risk assessment in action. Minnesota Law Rev 103(1):303–384
21. Fiske A, Henningsen P, Buyx A (2019) Your robot therapist will see you now: ethical implications of embodied artificial intelligence in psychiatry, psychology, and psychotherapy. J Medical Internet Res 21(5)
22. Khawaja Z, Bélisle-Pipon J-C (2023) Your robot therapist is not your therapist: understanding the role of AI-powered mental health chatbots. Front Dig Health 5:1278186
23. Payne K (2025) An AI chatbot pushed a teen to kill himself, a lawsuit against its creator alleges—apnews.com. https://apnews.com/article/chatbot-ai-lawsuit-suicide-teen-artificial-intelligence-9d48adc572100822fdbc3c90d1456bd0. [Accessed 06 Nov 2025]
24. Shinkoda P, Kao G (2021) Media bears responsibility for reinforcing Asian American stereotypes (Guest Column)—variety.com. https://variety.com/2021/film/news/media-asian-american-stereotypes-1234949658, 2021. [Accessed 06 Nov 2025]
25. Noble SU (2018) Algorithms of oppression: how search engines reinforce racism. NYU Press
26. Ross K, Carter C (2011) Women and news: a long and winding road. Media Cult Soc 33(8):1148–1165
27. Tuchman G (200) The symbolic annihilation of women by the mass media. Palgrave Macmillan US, New York, pp 150–174
28. Buolamwini J, Gebru T (2018) Gender shades: intersectional accuracy disparities in commercial gender classification. In: Friedler SA, Wilson C (eds) Proceedings of the 1st conference on fairness, accountability and transparency, vol 81 of Proceedings of machine learning research. PMLR, pp 77–91
29. Garg N, Schiebinger L, Jurafsky D, Zou J (2018) Word embeddings quantify 100 years of gender and ethnic stereotypes. Proc Natl Acad Sci 115(16):E3635–E3644
30. Papakyriakopoulos O, Mboya AM (2023) Beyond algorithmic bias: a socio-computational interrogation of the google search by image algorithm. Soc Sci Comput Rev 41(4):1100–1125
31. Sweeney L (2013) Discrimination in online ad delivery. Commun ACM 56(5):44–54
32. Kay M, Matuszek C, Munson SA (2015) Unequal representation and gender stereotypes in image search results for occupations. In: Proceedings of the 33rd annual ACM conference on human factors in computing systems, CHI '15, New York, NY, USA, pp 3819–3828. Association for Computing Machinery
33. Lam O, Wojcik S, Hughes A, Broderick B (2019) Men appear twice as often as women in news photos on facebook. Technical report, Pew Research Center
34. Otterbacher J, Bates J, Clough P (2017) Competent men and warm women: gender stereotypes and backlash in image search results. In: Proceedings of the 2017 CHI conference on human factors in computing systems, CHI '17, New York, NY, USA, pp 6620–6631. Association for Computing Machinery
35. Joachims T, Granka L, Pan B, Hembrooke H, Gay G (2005) Accurately interpreting click-through data as implicit feedback. In: Proceedings of the 28th annual international ACM SIGIR Conference on Research and Development in Information Retrieval, SIGIR '05, pp 154–161, New York, NY, USA, 2005. Association for Computing Machinery
36. Kulshrestha J, Eslami M, Messias J, Zafar MB, Ghosh S, Gummadi KP, Karahalios K (2019) Search bias quantification: investigating political bias in social media and web search. Inf Retr 22(1–2):188–227
37. Epstein R, Robertson RE (2015) The search engine manipulation effect (SEME) and its possible impact on the outcomes of elections. Proc Natl Acad Sci 112(33):E4512–E4521
38. Renström EA, Bäck H, Knapton HM (2020) Exploring a pathway to radicalization: the effects of social exclusion and rejection sensitivity. Group Proc Intergroup Relati 23(8):1204–1229
39. Hollewell GF, Longpré N (2022) Radicalization in the social media era: Understanding the relationship between self-radicalization and the internet. Int J Offender Ther Comp Criminol 66(8):896–913 PMID: 34189982

40. Mølmen GN, Ravndal JA (2023) Mechanisms of online radicalisation: how the internet affects the radicalisation of extreme-right lone actor terrorists. Behav Sci Terror Polit Aggress 15(4):463–487
41. Ribeiro MH, Ottoni R, West R, Virgílio AF (2020) Almeida, and Wagner Meira. Auditing radicalization pathways on YouTube. In: Proceedings of the 2020 conference on fairness, accountability, and transparency, FAT* '20, New York, NY, USA, pp 131–141. Association for Computing Machinery
42. Day M (2025) Curious LinkedIn search results highlight tech's diversity problems—seattletimes.com. https://www.seattletimes.com/business/microsoft/how-linkedins-search-engine-may-reflect-a-bias/. [Accessed 05 Nov 2025]
43. Baraniuk C (2025) LinkedIn denies gender bias claim over site search—bbc.com. https://www.bbc.com/news/technology-37306828, 2016. [Accessed 06 Nov 2025]
44. Dwork C, Hardt M, Pitassi T, Reingold O, Zemel R (2012) Fairness through awareness. In: Proceedings of the 3rd innovations in theoretical computer science conference, ITCS '12, New York, NY, USA, pp 214–226. Association for Computing Machinery
45. Hooker S (2021) Moving beyond "algorithmic bias is a data problem". Patterns (New York, N.Y.) 2(4):100241
46. Greenwald AG, McGhee DE, Schwartz JLK (1998) Measuring individual differences in implicit cognition: the implicit association test. J Personal Soc Psychol 74(6):1464
47. Bertrand M, Mullainathan S (2033) Are emily and greg more employable than Lakisha and Jamal? A Field Experiment on Labor Market Discrimination. Working Paper 9873, National Bureau of Economic Research, July 2003
48. Jakobson R, Waugh LR, Monville-Burston M (1995) On Language. Harvard University Press
49. Nosek BA, Banaji MR, Greenwald AG (2002) Harvesting implicit group attitudes and beliefs from a demonstration web site. Group Dynam 6(1):101–115
50. Bolukbasi T, Chang K-W, Zou J, Saligrama V, Kalai A (2016) Man is to computer programmer as woman is to homemaker? debiasing word embeddings. In: Proceedings of the 30th international conference on neural information processing systems, NIPS'16, pp 4356–4364, Red Hook, NY, USA, 2016. Curran Associates Inc
51. Pennington J, Socher R, Manning CD (2014) GloVe: global vectors for word representation. In: Empirical methods in natural language processing (EMNLP), PP 1532–1543
52. van Zoonen L (1998) A professional, unreliable, heroic marionette (m/f: Structure, agency and subjectivity in contemporary journalisms. Eur J Cult Stud 1(1):123–143
53. Caliskan A, Bryson JJ, Narayanan A (2017) Semantics derived automatically from language corpora contain human-like biases. Science 356(6334):183–186
54. Kosinski M, Stillwell D, Graepel T (2013) Private traits and attributes are predictable from digital records of human behavior. Proc Natl Acad Sci 110(15):5802–5805
55. Baeza-Yates R (2018) Bias on the web. Commun ACM 61(6):54–61
56. Chaney AJB, Stewart BM, Engelhardt BE (2018) How algorithmic confounding in recommendation systems increases homogeneity and decreases utility. In: Proceedings of the 12th ACM conference on recommender systems, RecSys '18, New York, NY, USA, pp 224–232. Association for Computing Machinery
57. Jiang R, Chiappa S, Lattimore T, György A, Kohli P (2019) Degenerate feedback loops in recommender systems. In: Proceedings of the 2019 AAAI/ACM conference on AI, ethics, and society, New York, NY, USA, pp 383–390. ACM
58. Amnesty (2025) Myanmar: facebook's systems promoted violence against Rohingya; Meta owes reparations—new report—amnesty.org. https://www.amnesty.org/en/latest/news/2022/09/myanmar-facebooks-systems-promoted-violence-against-rohingya-meta-owes-reparations-new-report/. [Accessed 06 Nov 2025]
59. de Guzman C (2022) Report: facebook algorithms promoted anti-rohingya violence—time.com. https://time.com/6217730/myanmar-meta-rohingya-facebook/. [Accessed 06 Nov 2025]
60. Roose K (2017) Forget washington. Facebook's problems abroad are far more disturbing. (Published 2017)—nytimes.com. https://www.nytimes.com/2017/10/29/business/facebook-misinformation-abroad.html. [Accessed 06 Nov 2025]

61. Mozur P (2018) A genocide incited on facebook, with posts from Myanmar's military (Published 2018)—nytimes.com. https://www.nytimes.com/2018/10/15/technology/myanmar-facebook-genocide.html. [Accessed 06 Nov 2025]
62. Rajagopalan M (2017) Internet trolls are using facebook to target Myanmar's Muslims—buzzfeednews.com. https://www.buzzfeednews.com/article/meghara/how-fake-news-and-online-hate-are-making-life-hell-for. [Accessed 06 Nov 2025
63. Bulut D (2023) The association between attention impairments and the internet and social media usage among adolescents and young adults with potential consequences: a review of literature. Psychology 14(8):1310–1321
64. Haidt J (2024) The anxious generation: how the great rewiring of childhood is causing an epidemic of mental illness. Penguin Press
65. Seabrook EM, Kern ML, Rickard NS (2016) Social networking sites, depression, and anxiety: a systematic review. JMIR Ment Health 3(4):e50

Chapter 3
Measuring Unfairness

Abstract Information retrieval systems may often deliver biased or unfair results, and before one can mitigate such unfairness, one must first measure it. In this chapter, we consider a number of information retrieval methods, and discuss metrics to measure the fairness of the output from such methods. We begin with a discussion of word embeddings, which represent terms as numerical vectors and are often used in downstream applications. Many popular word embeddings are known to exhibit undesirable bias, including gender bias. We then discuss search result ranking, in which bias may result in certain demographic groups being overrepresented or underrepresented.

3.1 Introduction

IR systems play a crucial role in delivering relevant information to the end users. However, as discussed in Chap. 2, these systems can reflect and even amplify historic and existing societal biases present in the data or learned through algorithmic process. This can lead to unequal, unfair representations and exposure of groups in the results delivered by the IR systems.

Measuring unfairness is an important step in understanding extent of biased results and to make information retrieval fairer for future use. In this chapter, we describe approaches to detect and quantify bias. First, in numerical vectors that make word embeddings and then in ranked list of outputs from IR systems.

Section 3.2 reviews techniques for detecting and measuring biases in word embeddings. Section 3.3 introduces fairness metrics needed to identify bias in ranked outputs from IR systems.

3.2 Bias in Word Embeddings

Word embeddings transform text data into vector representations that serve as input for downstream tasks such as machine translation, sentiment analysis and information retrieval. These models learn meaningful word representation by analyzing patterns of word co-occurences in text corpora. The process is repeated for all words in the vocabulary to produce a matrix representation of the input data. However, these embeddings inherit biases present in the training data. Bolukbasi et al. [1] and Caliskan et al. [2] demonstrated that word embeddings contain systematic biases that mirror harmful associations present in the language. In the following sections we discuss various methods to detect and measure these biases in word embeddings.

3.2.1 Detecting Bias in Word Embeddings

Bias in word embeddings can be detected through exploratory analysis, as demonstrated by Bolukbasi et al. [1]. They compiled the list of occupations closest to gendered words such as *she* and *he* in the embeddings, and then tasked crowdworkers with associating each occupation as neutral, female-centric, or male-centric. The observed gender leaning of occupations, as determined by similarity measures strongly aligned with the crowdworkers judgment.

Another method is to adapt analogy tasks to reveal bias. Normally, analogies evaluate pairs such as 'man is to king as woman is to queen'. The analogy task is modified for gender association test, such that it uses 2 seed words (a, b): (*she, he*; *woman, man*, and so on) and evaluates different pairs of candidate target pairs (x, y): (e.g., *nurse,doctor*). A bias score can be defined as:

$$S_{(a,b)}(x, y) = \cos\left(\mathbf{a} - \mathbf{b}, \mathbf{x} - \mathbf{y}\right),$$

where $\mathbf{w}$ denotes the embedding vector for word w. One may further restrict evaluation to pairs where $\|\mathbf{x} - \mathbf{y}\| \leq \delta$, ensuring that only semantically related pairs are compared. Higher absolute scores indicate stronger alignment of the target pair's relationship with the gendered seed pair.

3.2.2 Measuring Bias in Word Embeddings

Bolukbasi et al. [1] introduced a method to quantify gender bias in word embeddings by detecting a gender subspace. First, multiple gender word pairs are collected, such as *she,he; woman, man; girl, boy*, etc. For each pair w_f, w_m the vector difference $\mathbf{w_f} - \mathbf{w_m}$ is is measured. Averaging these differences yield an estimated gender direction:

$$\mathbf{g} \in \mathbb{R}^d,$$

where d is the embedding dimension.

To measure the bias, one can iterate through a set of neutral words to quantify the extent to which bias is present in the embeddings. If neutral words are more closely associated with one gender group, then it can signal the presence of bias. More concretely, if there are total N gender-neutral words and using $\mathbf{g}$, bias is defined as:

$$Bias = \frac{1}{N} \sum_{w \in N} |\cos(\mathbf{w}, \mathbf{g})|^c,$$

where c is a tuning parameter. If $c = 0$, then $\cos(\mathbf{w}, \mathbf{g})$ is 1 for all non-zero cosine values. If c is 1, then bias is aggregated linearly. If the embedding is unbiased, then neutral words will be equidistant from both gender-specific words resulting in low bias scores.

3.2.3 Word Embedding Association Test

Caliskan et al. [2] proposed the *Word Embedding Association Test (WEAT)* to measure the relative association of a set of target words (e.g. scientist, programmer; librarian, nurse), with a set of attribute words (e.g. man, male; woman, female). The association of target words with attribute words is measured as:

$$s(X, Y, A, B) = \sum_{x \in X} s(x, A, B) - \sum_{y \in Y} s(y, A, B),$$

where X and Y are sets of target words and A, B are sets of attribute words. For a word w, we have:

$$s(w, A, B) = mean_{a \in A} \cos(\mathbf{w}, \mathbf{a}) - mean_{b \in B} \cos(\mathbf{w}, \mathbf{b}).$$

$s(w, A, B)$ measures the association of a word with a target word, and similarly $s(X, Y, A, B)$ measures the association of a set of target words with association words. One can then measure the p-value of the test as $Pr[s(X_i, Y_i, A, B) > s(X, Y, A, B)]$, where $Pr[X_i, Y_i]$ is the set of all permutations of $X \cup Y$ into two sets of equal size. The method calculate all instances where a random permutation has more s-score than the observed statistic from actual X, Y. If the result is small ($p < 0.05$) then it suggests that the result is statistically significant.

The separation between the target and attribute distributions with effect size is measured as:

$$\frac{mean_{a \in A} \cos(\mathbf{w}, \mathbf{a}) - mean_{b \in B} \cos(\mathbf{w}, \mathbf{b})}{std Dev_{w \in X \cup Y} s(w, A, B)}.$$

3.2.4 Bias Detection for Gendered Languages

The methodology proposed by Bolukbasi et al. [1], described in Sect. 3.2.2, uses a cosine distance between a word vector $\mathbf{w}$ and the gender subspace vector $\mathbf{g}$. It relies on a belief that neutral words such as *nurse* should be equidistant from gender specific words such as (*man, woman; male, female; he, she;* etc.) and any deviation from the gender subspace is identified as *bias*.

Papakyriakopoulos et al. [3] examined word embedding bias in case of languages where words are gendered. For example, in German, *Krankenschwester* is used for a female nurse and *Krankenpfleger* for a male nurse. Unlike the Bolukbasi et al. [1] methods discussed above, in gendered languages, the neutral words should be equidistant to the gender directions and the gendered word vector should be dependent on it's gender direction.

Papakyriakopoulos et al. [3] use theory-specific words for each type of discrimination, such as (*man, woman*) for sexism, (*German, foreigners*) for xenophobia, and (*straight, gay*) for homophobic prejudices. They also define a list of concepts to measure bias. If a word is gendered and has male and female versions then they are represented by a word-pairs. The method measures bias in word embeddings as:

$$B_g = \frac{1}{NK} \sum_{i=1}^{N} \sum_{j=1}^{K} |\cos(w_{j1}, P_{n1}) - \cos(w_{j2}, P_{n2})|,$$

where N is the number of concepts, K is number of theory specific pairs, w_{j1}, w_{j2} are the embeddings for the jth pair of theory-specific words, and P_{n1}, P_{n2} are embeddings for the nth pair of concepts in the list. When a word does not have gender-specific names ($P_{n1} = P_{n2}$), then a single word vector is used as shown below:

$$B_g = \frac{1}{NK} \sum_{i=1}^{N} \sum_{j=1}^{K} |\cos(w_{j1}, P_n) - \cos(w_{j2}, P_n)|.$$

3.3 Measuring Unfairness in Ranked Results

Ranking-based information retrieval systems are a fundamental component of web-based search engines, recommender systems, and social media platforms. These systems take a user query and return a ranked list of items based on estimated relevance. For example, Google search returns a list of web pages for a given query, e-commerce platforms like Amazon rank products based on user browsing history, and social media platforms like Instagram recommend a list of content based on predicted engagement.

However, these systems can unintentionally favor certain groups or disadvantage others. For example, an image search platform might consistently rank images from certain groups higher than others. Women are often underrepresented in image search results for occupations such as bill collector, general manager, and chief executive, and overrepresented in certain occupations' image search results, such as singer, computer programmer, and model [4]. E-commerce platforms may systematically promote products from certain brands or price ranges in their search rankings [5].

This can lead to unequal and unfair representation or exposure of some groups in ranked outputs. Addressing this challenge requires an understanding of fairness concepts, methods to evaluate unfairness in results, and ways to mitigate the biases (see Chapter 5).

Dwork et al. defined multiple fairness factors for use in designing classification algorithms, many of which extend naturally to IR systems [6].

Individual Fairness asks that similar individuals (or items) should be treated similarly, irrespective of their group membership. For an IR task, similarity can be defined with respect to relevance to a query. Given a set of items, where each item is associated as a member of protected or majority group, **group fairness** requires similar outcomes for different groups. *Statistical parity* demands that the proportion of protected-group items in the output matches that of the population. However, statistical parity alone is inadequate, as a system can decide to recommend same items from one group irrespective of users demand; indicating lack of diversity in items from one group.

Beyond individual and group fairness, IR systems often involve multiple stakeholders. These perspectives are defined as providers, consumers, or both [7]. In such multi-stakeholder recommender systems, the following concepts may be used.

1. **C-fairness (Consumer Fairness)** Requires that all consumers have access to relevant items.
2. **P-fairness (Provider Fairness)** Requires that the providers/items on the system reach all users. This metric aims at avoiding monopolies and popularity bias, and ensures that content from new providers gets visibility on the platform. It requires a balance in the returned list of items to make sure it contains results from dominant and minority groups.
3. **CP-fairness (Consumer-Provider fairness)** The third category takes both consumers and providers into account. As in case of the hiring platform example, the platform can require that minority job seekers have similar visibility on the platform as the majority counterparts. Similarly, the platform can require that minority employers receive the same quality of candidates as the employers from the majority class.

To address such concerns and make IR systems fair, we begin by establishing two key steps:

1. Evaluating Fairness: Quantify the degree of unfairness in a given ranking.
2. Loss Objectives: Create algorithms that mitigate bias as evaluated in Step 1 (see Chaps. 4 and 5).

Notation. In this and the upcoming chapters, we use the following notation: Given an information retrieval system (such as a search engine) S, a collection of documents (or items) D, and a query q, the system S returns a ranked list of results L in response to a query q. Each document d may be associated with $g \geq 1$ groups. The group alignment for a document d is defined as $G(d) \in [0, 1]^g$. $G^+(L)$ denotes the set of documents in the target protected group and $G^-(L)$ denotes the set of

Table 3.1 Summary of notations

S	Information retrieval system
D	Database of documents
q	Search query
$d \in D$	Documents in D
L	Ranked list of N documents
$L(d)$	Rank of document d in list L
g	number of groups
$G(L)$	Group alignment matrix
$G(d)$	Group alignment for a document d
$G^+(L)$	Set of documents in L associated with target group
$G^-(L)$	Set of documents in L not associated with target group
$\hat{\mathbf{p}}$	Target distribution
$\mathbf{a_L}$	Attention vector for documents in L
$\mathbf{a_L(d)}$	Attention vector for documents in L
ϵ_L	Exposure of groups in L

remaining documents. We assume only one target protected group, but many of the approaches that we discuss can be generalized to multiple such groups.

Given N returned documents in ranked list L and g groups, an $(N \times g)$ binary group alignment matrix $G(L)$ is created. $\hat{\mathbf{p}}$ represents the ideal or target group distribution for L. In a ranked list L, documents at top positions receive much more attention or exposure then lower ranked documents. For example, lower ranked documents receive geometrically low user attention while relevance of the document decreases in a linear order as noted by Biega et al. [8]. This position bias is used by metrics to account for how much user interaction, a ranked document may receive. If we denote a $\mathbf{a_L}$ as attention vector for the list L, then attention weight for a document is defined by $\mathbf{a_L(d)}$. Similarly, exposure across groups is defined by the use of the position of the documents in a ranked list L with their respective group associations $G(L)$, $\epsilon_L = L(G(L)^T \mathbf{a_L})$.

We use notations similar to Raj and Ekstrand [9], summarized in Table 3.1.

In following discussion we use mathematical description as described in the original work, followed by a discussion on definitions and implementation methods.

We now describe various metrics that can be used to inform algorithmic design.

3.3.1 Rank Aware Statistical Parity Measures

Statistical parity refers to the requirement that the group distribution of items receiving a particular treatment should be identical to the demographics of the population as a whole [6, 10].

Yang and Stoyanovich evaluated a ranking scheme that exhibits statistical parity, reflecting the idea that the item's position in a ranked list should not be related to the item's membership in a protected group. They present three measures based on above definition of statistical parity. They include the effects of position bias in the ranking measures by using a logarithmic discounting method similar to $nDCG$ [11]. This allows the measures to give more importance to items that are ranked at higher positions. Proposed measures are normalized between [0, 1] with being most 1 being most unfair and 0 being the most fair value [12].

This method assumes that items can only belong to one protected group at a time, and membership is binary. Each item can either belong to the majority group or the minority group.

Yang and Stoyanovich proposed three fairness measures:

Normalized discounted difference (rND). This measure computes the difference in proportion of members of the protected group at top-i positions and in the overall population. For a given ranked list L:

$$rND(L) = \frac{1}{Z} \sum_{i=10,20,\dots}^{N} \frac{1}{\log_2 i} \left| \frac{|G_{1\dots i}^+|}{i} - \frac{|G^+|}{N} \right|.$$

N is the total number of items in L and the group of interest is defined as G^+. The difference in the proportions is accumulated at discrete ranking points, weighted by a logarithmic discount. Normalizer Z is the maximum possible weighted sum of differences in proportions, where the weights are inverse logarithms of the position cutoffs. The maximum value for Z is when the ranking is most unfair, when all items from group G^+ are assumed to be either at the top or bottom of a ranking.

rND is a convex and continuous measure but not differentiable, limiting its use in optimization procedures.

Normalized discounted KL-divergence (rKL). This measure uses KL-divergence to find the divergence between probability distribution of the two groups at the top-i ranking vs. in the overall ranking (ranking L has N documents). The Kullback-Leibler (KL) divergence is used to compute how one probability distribution is different than the other:

$$D_{KL}(P||Q) = \sum_i P(i) \log \frac{P(i)}{Q(i)},$$

where P and Q are two probability distributions.

rKL is defined as:

$$P = \left(\frac{|G^+_{1\ldots i}|}{i}, \frac{|G^-_{1\ldots i}|}{i}\right), \; Q = \left(\frac{G^+}{N}, \frac{|G^-|}{N}\right),$$

$$rKL(L) = \frac{1}{Z} \sum_{i=10,20,\ldots}^{N} \frac{D_{KL}(P\|Q)}{\log_2 i},$$

Here, Z is the normalizer, as described above.

rKL provides a benefit in that it can be extended to more than two groups without modification.

Normalized discounted ratio (rRD). rRD uses the ratio of the size of G^+ with the size of G^- items at top-i positions and in the overall population:

$$rRD(L) = \frac{1}{Z} \sum_{i=10,20,\ldots}^{N} \frac{1}{\log_2 i} \left| \frac{|G^+_{1\ldots i}|}{|G^-_{1\ldots i}|} - \frac{|G^+|}{|G^-|} \right|.$$

rRD is only applied when the target group G^+ is also the minority group.

3.3.2 FAIR Metric

Unlike the methods in Sect. 3.3.1, *FAIR* focuses on representation at prefix levels $L_{\leq k}$, ensuring that group, G^+ is not under-represented at different levels of the ranking. Raj and Ekstrand modified the constraints proposed in the *FAIR* algorithm to design a metric [9, 13]:

$$FAIR(L) = \frac{1}{N} \sum_{k=1}^{N} \sum_{j=1}^{G^+(L_{\leq k})} \binom{k}{j} (\hat{\mathbf{p}})^j (1 - \hat{\mathbf{p}})^{k-j}.$$

The *FAIR* algorithm is based on statistical parity and group fairness. It creates two queues P_0, P_1 for candidate items from G^+ and G^- groups. For each rank, it calculates the number of candidates from each group that are required and uses a greedy approach to create a fair ranked list. *FAIR* only works for binomial groups and single ranked list [13].

3.3.3 Viable-Λ Test

Sapiezynski et al. proposed the Viable-Λ Test, which incorporates user attention for position bias instead of logarithmic discounts [14]. They argue against using logarithmic discount methods, such as $nDCG$, as it is a slow decay function. First page search results get much more attention then results on later pages, which leads to a much sharp attention decline then what logarithmic decay accounts for. The authors mention other methods such as Truncated Geometric Distribution, Truncated Log-series Distribution, and Truncated Discrete Pareto Distribution that can be used to model attention weights [15].

The metric requires five design components:

1. Alignment vector: Given a ranking L, and groups g, one can define the group alignment for a document d in L as $G(d)$ and the alignment vector G_L for the list L.
2. Attentional weight vector: The attentional weight vector accounts for discounted user attention for each item $L_i \in L$. As the property cannot be known beforehand, but it can be modeled in terms of click-through rates (CTR) received by items, or even by eye tracking methods. In an algorithmic setup where user feedback is not available, a discrete truncated probability distribution can be used, such as Truncated Geometric Distribution, with the condition that items at higher ranks should receive much more attention than the lower ranked items: $\mathbf{a}_{L_1} \gg \mathbf{a}_{L_i}$ as $i \to N$ for a reasonably large n.

   If $\mathbf{a}_L$ is the attention weight given to each item $L_i \in R$ based on an user attention function, then the expected cumulative exposure ϵ_L is defined as:

$$\epsilon_{\mathbf{L}} = G_L^T \cdot \mathbf{a}_{\mathbf{L}}.$$

3. Population estimator: Similar to metrics discussed previously, target demographic distribution or extracted true demographic proportions as probability distributions is denoted by $\hat{\mathbf{p}}$.
4. Distance metric d: The distance metric is a statistical difference metric that measures the difference between probability distributions ϵ_L and $\hat{\mathbf{p}}$.
5. Maximum acceptable distance δ_{max}: This a threshold value that defines acceptable values around $\hat{\mathbf{p}}$, such that if d is within the threshold then group fairness is preserved.

These design components are combined into a metric, known as Attention-Weighted Rank Fairness (AWRF) [9].

$$AWRF_\Delta(L) = \Delta(\epsilon_{\mathbf{L}}, \hat{\mathbf{p}}).$$

The metric combines exposure distribution ϵ_L with the target estimator $\hat{\mathbf{p}}$. Δ can be chosen depending on the task: similar to previous methods, it can be a normalized difference or a discounted ratio if the groups are binomial. KL-divergence can be used for soft associations and multinomial protected attributes.

3.3.4 Exposure-Based Fair Rankings

The methods discussed in Sects. 3.3.1, 3.3.2, and 3.3.3 aim to maintain statistical
parity in single rankings. It is possible that, on some occasions, a single ranking can
not deliver fair results, and multiple rankings are needed. A way to achieve fairness
across multiple ranking is to measure exposure of results returned for a query over a
distribution of rankings.

The exposure based framework focuses on fairness constraints in rankings in
terms of exposure allocation, where exposure is mostly determined by the position
in the ranked list. Singh and Joachims [16] expressed exposure under probabilistic
ranking P as:

$$Exposure(d_i|P) = \sum_{j=1}^{N} P_{i,j} v_j,$$

where v_j represents position bias at j and $P_{i,j}$ is the probability that document d_i is
at rank j.

Demographic Parity (DP). Measures the difference in average exposure of the
two groups. The metric assumes presence of only two groups G^+ and G^-.

$$Exposure(G^+|P) = Exposure(G^+|P).$$

Here,

$$Exposure(G^k|P) = \frac{1}{|G^k|} \sum_{d_i \in G^k} Exposure(d_i|P).$$

The demographic parity metric is then defined as:

$$DP = \frac{Exposure(G^+|P)}{Exposure(G^-|P)}$$

Disparate Treatment Ratio (DTR). If the average utility of a group is defined
as:

$$U(G_k|q) = \frac{1}{|G^k|} \sum_{d_i \in G^k} u_i,$$

where the query is defined by q. The constraint enforces that the exposure of the
documents for both groups should be proportional to the utility:

$$\frac{Exposure(G^+|P)}{U(G^+|q)} = \frac{Exposure(G^-|P)}{U(G^-|q)},$$

$$DTR(G^+, G^-|P, q) = \frac{Exposure(G^+|P)/U(G^+|q)}{Exposure(G^-|P)/U(G^-|q)}.$$

Both groups are treated equally if $DTR = 1$. It is less than 1 if group G^- is favored and more than 1 if G^+ is treated better than G^-.

Disparate Impact Ratio (DIR). Ensures that users are interacting with items from different groups proportionally: i.e., the average click through rate for each group is proportional. $P(\text{click document i}) = Exposure(d_i) \times P(\text{i is relevant})$, $P(\text{click document i}) = \sum_{j=1}^{N} P_{i,j} v_j \times u_i$.

Disparate impact ensures that the click through rate is proportional to average utility for both groups,

$$\frac{CTR(G^+|P)}{U(G^+|P)} = \frac{CTR(G^-|P)}{U(G^-|P)}.$$

Disparate Impact Ratio (DIR) is defined as

$$DIR(G^+, G^-, |P, q) = \frac{CTR(G^+|P)/U(G^+|q)}{CTR(G^-|P)/U(G^-|q)}.$$

Similar to DTR, a DIR less than 1 or greater than 1 signifies which group is favored in the ranking.

3.3.5 Equity of Amortized Attention

Biega et al. defined *Equity of Amortized Attention* for a set of rankings. If each item receives cumulative attention proportional to their cumulative relevance, then the set of rankings delivers *equity of amortized attention*, or *EAA* [8]. Attention here refers to position bias, as attention paid to items is strongly linked with position of the item in the ranking. For total m rankings, where a, r refer to attention and relevance received by items in different rankings, the ratio of cumulated attention to relevance should be same for different items:

$$\frac{\sum_{j=1}^{m} a_{L_j}(d_1)}{\sum_{j=1}^{m} r_{L_j}(d_1)} = \frac{\sum_{j=1}^{m} a_{L_j}(d_2)}{\sum_{j=1}^{m} r_{L_j}(d_2)}, \forall d_1, d_2.$$

One can permute a ranking over time, making sure an item receives optimal attention subject to its relevance score [8]. *IAA*, or *inequity of amortized attention* [9], is an unfairness score that measures how far a sequence of ranking $L_1, L_2, \ldots, L_m$ has deviated from fairness criteria as defined by *EAA*.

$$IAA = \sum_{i=1}^{n} |A_i - R_i| = \sum_{i=1}^{n} \left| \sum_{j=1}^{m} a_{L_j}(d_i) - \sum_{j=1}^{m} r_{L_j}(d_i) \right|.$$

IAA values closer to 0 signify that attention distribution of items are closer to their relevance values, accumulated over a set of rankings. Larger values highlight unfairness.

3.3.6   Expected Exposure

Similar to *EAA* (Section 3.3.5), Diaz et al. defined the principle of *equal expected exposure: Given a fixed information need, no item should be exposed (in expectation) more or less than any other item of the same relevance* [17].

Target exposure. Consider availability of an oracle which provides optimal rankings at random. Where any relevant item can be ranked at position $0 \leq i < m$, where there are total m relevant documents. All relevant items receive same exposure in expectation, similarly non relevant items also receive the same exposure in expectation. Target exposure ϵ^* is the expected exposure of all items under the oracle policy.

Computing expected and target exposure. Diaz et al. uses user browsing models such as *rank-biased precision* and *expected reciprocal rank* to compute expected ϵ and target exposures ϵ^*.

Rank-biased precision (RBP). It is a metric based on an assumption that probability of visiting a document decreases with rank [18].

$$RBP(\sigma) = (1 - \gamma) \sum_{i \in [0,k)]} \mathbf{y}^*_{\sigma_i} \gamma^i,$$

where $\mathbf{y}^*$ is a binary relevance vector, k is the maximum browsing depth and γ is the patience parameter. The expected exposure of a document d is defined as:

$$\epsilon_d = \sum_{\sigma \in S_n} \pi(\sigma | q) \gamma^{\hat{\sigma}_d},$$

where the expected exposure ϵ is computed for an arbitrary policy π. $\hat{\sigma}$ is the map from document indexes to ranks. S_n is set of all permutations of size n, n is the size of total documents in the corpus.

For an oracle policy, one can compute target exposure ϵ^* as:

$$\epsilon_d^* = \frac{1}{m} \sum_{i \in [0,m)} \gamma^i,$$

where each relevant document is randomly selected, each relevant document can occur at each of the top-m positions equally.

The squared error between expected and target exposure can be used to find the deviation between equal expected exposure and target exposure:

$$EEL = l(\epsilon, \epsilon^*) = ||\epsilon - \epsilon^*||_2^2 = ||\epsilon||_2^2 - 2\epsilon^T \epsilon^* + ||\epsilon^*||_2^2 \qquad (3.1)$$

$$= |\epsilon||_2^2 - 2\epsilon^T \epsilon^* + ||\epsilon^*||_2^2.$$

Here, the expected exposure disparity (EE-D): $||\epsilon||_2^2$, measures inequalities in the exposure distribution. Expected exposure relevance (EE-R): $2\epsilon^T \epsilon^*$ quantifies exposure on relevant documents.

3.3.7 Skew@k Measure

Geyik et al. proposed a measure for use at LinkedIn, incorporating fairness-aware measures into the search system. They present two evaluation measures to judge the bias of results [19]. Note that in this measure, we define attribute value for i_{th} document as a_i, not to be confused with attention weight vector for a ranking $\mathbf{a_L}$.

1. Measure based on top-k Results: This measure calculates the skewness of the ranking L, given a search query q for an attribute value a_i:

$$Skew_{a_i}@k(L) = \log_e \left(\frac{P_{L,q,a_i}}{P_{D,q,a_i}} \right).$$

   $Skew_{a_i}@k$ is the logarithmic ratio between proportion of candidates in L that have the attribute value a_i to the desired proportion of candidates D for request q. For example, considering the gender attribute, suppose that for a given job listing, LinkedIn has a set of total qualified candidates as $20K$ males and $40K$ females. So, the desired ratios are : $P_{D,q,male} = 0.33$ and $P_{D,q,female} = 0.66$. If the top-100 ranked results for the task contain 5 male candidates and 95 female candidates, then the $skew_{male}@100 = \log_e \frac{5/100}{20K/(20K+40K)} = \log_e(0.15) = -1.897$. The negative ratio signifies a less-than-desired representation. The $Skew_{a_i}@k$ measure is easy to interpret but it only works for one attribute at a time with a fixed k. To fully analyze rankings, one must vary k and evaluate rankings with different attributes to understand biased results.
2. Ranking Measure: This measure uses Normalized Kullback-Leibler (KL) divergence to understand how far the attribute distribution of top-k results is to the total attribute distribution for a query q:

$$NDKL(L_q) = \frac{1}{Z} \sum_{i=1}^{|L|} \frac{1}{\log_2(i+1)} d_{kl}(D_{L_q^i} || D_q).$$

   Here, L_q is the top-k ranking of results for a search query q, $\frac{1}{Z}\sum_{i=1}^{|N|} \frac{1}{\log_2(i+1)}$ accounts for position bias for each result in $|L|$, $D_{L_q^i}$ is the attribute distribution of i_{th} ranked item, and D_q is the attribute distribution of all possible result candidates for the search query q. This measure is more difficult to interpret, but it can handle multiple attributes and also provides a single bias value for the top-k results to understand fair or unfairness of the ranking (Table 3.2).

Table 3.2 Summary of fair ranking metrics

Metric	Group Membership	Goal	Comments
rND [12]	Binomial	Measures group memberships difference at top-i ranking and in the overall population	–
rKL [12]	Multinomial	Measures probability distribution divergence of the groups at top-i ranking and in the overall population	Useful when items belong to binary (binomial) or multiple (multinomial) groups
rRD [12]	Binomial	Measures group memberships difference for protected and the majority group at top-i ranking	Only applicable when protected group is atmost half of the population
FAIR [13]	Binomial	Ensures the target group is not under-represented at different levels of ranking	–
AWRF [14]	Depends on the comparing function	Compares exposure to items in a ranking with target proportions. Uses user attention for position bias instead of logarithmic decay	–
DP [16]	Binomial	Measures average exposure received by the two groups	Exposure of results over multiple rankings
DTR [16]	Binomial	Forces the exposure of the two groups to be proportional to the utility	
DIR [16]	Binomial	Ensures click through rate for each group is proportional	
IAA [8]	Multinomial	Measures divergence of sequence of rankings from target fairness criteria	Ratio of attention to relevance for different items across multiple rankings should be same
EEL [17]	Multinomial	Measures difference in expected exposure and target exposure	–
EER [17]	Multinomial	Evaluates exposure and relevance alignment	–
Skew@k [19]	Binomial	Measures logarithmic ratio of candidates with an attribute against target proportion of candidates with the same attribute	Works for one attribute at a time

Using these evaluation measures, one can implement greedy-based algorithms [19]. Given a desired target distribution of attribute values for the ranked list, one can greedily decide which items to include in the list given how well they satisfy the attribute requirements, ensuring that there is at least some minimum representation of each protected attribute in the top-k ranks. An implementation of this approach on LinkedIn led to improvement in fairness metrics, with a much better representation of protected attributes in ranked lists.

We refer the readers to [9, 20, 21] for detailed explanations on fairness evaluation measures.

References

1. Bolukbasi T, Chang K-W, Zou J, Saligrama V, Kalai A (2016) Man is to computer programmer as woman is to homemaker? Debiasing word embeddings. In: Proceedings of the 30th international conference on neural information processing systems, NIPS'16, Red Hook, NY, USA, pp 4356–4364. Curran Associates Inc
2. Jentzsch S, Schramowski P, Rothkopf C, Kersting K (2019) Semantics derived automatically from language corpora contain human-like moral choices. In: Proceedings of the 2019 AAAI/ACM conference on AI, ethics, and society, AIES '19, New York, NY, USA, pp 37–44. Association for Computing Machinery
3. Papakyriakopoulos O, Hegelich S, Serrano JCM, Marco F (2020) Bias in word embeddings. In: Proceedings of the 2020 conference on fairness, accountability, and transparency, FAT* '20, New York, NY, USA, pp 446–457. Association for Computing Machinery
4. Lam O, Wojcik S, Hughes A, Broderick B (2019) Men appear twice as often as women in news photos on facebook. Technical report, Pew Research Center
5. Fussell S (2019) Algorithms are people—theatlantic.com. https://www.theatlantic.com/technology/archive/2019/09/is-amazons-search-algorithm-biased-its-hard-to-prove/598264/. [Accessed 06 Nov 2025]
6. Dwork C, Hardt M, Pitassi T, Reingold O, Zemel R (2012) Fairness through awareness. In Proceedings of the 3rd innovations in theoretical computer science conference, ITCS '12, New York, NY, USA, pp 214–226. Association for Computing Machinery
7. Burke R (2017) Multisided fairness for recommendation. ArXiv preprint arXiv:1707.00093
8. Biega AJ, Gummadi KP, Weikum G (2018) Equity of attention: amortizing individual fairness in rankings. In: The 41st international ACM SIGIR conference on research and development in information retrieval, SIGIR '18, New York, NY, USA, pp 405–414. Association for Computing Machinery
9. Raj A, Ekstrand MD (2020) Comparing fair ranking metrics. ArXiv preprint arXiv:2009.01311
10. Friedler SA, Scheidegger C, Venkatasubramanian S (2021) The (im) possibility of fairness: different value systems require different mechanisms for fair decision making. Commun ACM 64(4):136–143
11. Järvelin K, Kekäläinen J (2002) Cumulated gain-based evaluation of IR techniques. ACM Trans Inf Syst 20(4):422–446
12. Yang K, Stoyanovich J (2017) Measuring fairness in ranked outputs. In: Proceedings of the 29th international conference on scientific and statistical database management, SSDBM '17, New York, NY, USA. Association for Computing Machinery
13. Zehlike M, Bonchi F, Castillo C, Hajian S, Megahed M, Baeza-Yates R (2017) FA*IR: A Fair Top-k ranking algorithm. In: Proceedings of the 2017 ACM on conference on information and knowledge management, CIKM '17, page 1569–1578, New York, NY, USA. Association for Computing Machinery

14. Sapiezynski P, Zeng W, Robertson RE, Mislove RE, Wilson C (2019) Quantifying the impact of user attention on fair group representation in ranked lists. In: Companion proceedings of the 2019 world wide web conference, WWW '19, New York, NY, USA, pp 553–562. Association for Computing Machinery
15. Kozubowski TJ, Panorska AK, Forister ML (2015) A discrete truncated Pareto distribution. Stat Methodol 26:135–150
16. Singh A, Joachims T (2018) Fairness of exposure in rankings. In: Proceedings of the 24th ACM SIGKDD international conference on knowledge discovery and data mining, KDD '18, New York, NY, USA, pp 2219–2228. Association for Computing Machinery
17. Diaz F, Mitra B, Ekstrand MD, Biega AJ, Carterette B (2020) Evaluating stochastic rankings with expected exposure. In: Proceedings of the 29th ACM international conference on information and knowledge management, CIKM '20, New York, NY, USA, pp 275–284. Association for Computing Machinery
18. Moffat A, Zobel J (2008) Rank-biased precision for measurement of retrieval effectiveness. ACM Trans Inf Syst 27(1)
19. Geyik SC, Ambler S, Kenthapadi K (2019) Fairness-aware ranking in search and recommendation systems with application to linkedin talent search. In: Proceedings of the 25th ACM SIGKDD international conference on knowledge discovery and data mining, KDD '19, New York, NY, USA, pp 2221–2231. Association for Computing Machinery
20. Raj A, Ekstrand MD (2022) Measuring fairness in ranked results: an analytical and empirical comparison. In: Proceedings of the 45th international ACM SIGIR conference on research and development in information retrieval, SIGIR '22, New York, NY, USA, pp 726–736. Association for Computing Machinery
21. Zehlike M, Yang K, Stoyanovich J (2021) Fairness in ranking: a survey. ArXiv preprint-arXiv:2103.14000

Chapter 4
Debiasing Word Embeddings

Abstract Word embeddings, which create a numerical representation of text data, are an important part of many information retrieval systems. These methods find application in tasks such as search, classification, and sentiment analysis. However, a number of studies have observed the presence of bias in embedding methods: famously, the word *woman* is closely associated with *nurse*, while *man* is associated with *doctor*. In this section, we discuss techniques to debias word embeddings, including both hard-debiasing, which removes the part of the vector representation that lies along a particular (e.g., gender) subspace, and soft-debiasing, which reduces the effect of a particular subspace.

4.1 Introduction

Word embeddings transform text data into numerical vectors, which serve as input in various machine learning algorithms for use cases such as web search, spam classification, sentiment analysis, and document parsing. Word embedding algorithms use surrounding words to learn a meaningful representation of the target word. The process is performed for all words in the corpus, resulting in a matrix representation of input data. The learned embeddings can then be used for various downstream applications as well as even for different use cases using transfer learning.

Word embeddings are a chapter in the long history of finding numerical representations of data that can be used as input to various statistical, ML, and deep learning-based models. Other such methods include traditional approaches such as one-hot encoding, *TF-IDF*, *LSA*, and *LDA* [1–3], and modern word embeddings based approaches like *word2vec*-based models such as *CBOW* and *skip-gram* [4], contextual representations models such as *BERT* [5], and generative pre-trained models such as *GPT* [6], all of which can be used to find numerical representations for text data. The choice of the appropriate encoding method depends on the scale of data available and the specific task.

H. Mishra and S. Soundarajan, *Addressing Bias in Information Retrieval*,
SpringerBriefs in Intelligent Systems, https://doi.org/10.1007/978-3-032-24145-0_4

4.2 Background

Machine learning models require the transformation of categorical data into a numerical representation for algorithmic processing. Ordinal encoding, which assigns sequential integers to categories, can be used for this task, but is only appropriate when categories contain an inherent ordering that can be suitably represented through ordered values. Many categorical data-types, such as product names, colors, and geo-locations, lack meaningful order, which renders ordinal encoding inappropriate for such tasks.

One-Hot Encoding addresses this limitation by creating a binary vector representation for categorical variables. This method transforms each categorical variable into multiple binary features, where each unique category becomes a separate column in the feature space. For each data instance, the encoding assigns a 1 to the new column if it contains the present category and 0 to all other category columns. This approach retains the independence of categorical features while providing the numerical input required for algorithms.

TF-IDF. *TF-IDF* addresses the limitations of one-hot encoding by measuring the importance of a single word t in a document d versus its relative importance with respect to other documents D [2]. Terms that occur more often within a document are considered more important indicators of the document's content. *TF*, or term frequency, is given by $tf(t, d)$ and measures how frequently a term t appears in a document d.

$$tf(t, d) = \frac{f_{t,d}}{\sum_{t' \in d} f_{t',d}}.$$

This is the ratio of the number of times a term appears in a document to the frequency of other terms in the document. Terms that occur frequently across many documents such as stop words are less useful for identifying relevant documents. The inverse document frequency, or *IDF*, of the term is used to down-weight the importance of a term if it is present in a large number of documents, and is given by

$$idf(t, D) = \log \frac{N}{|d \in D, t \in d|}.$$

TF-IDF combines these terms as:

$$tf - idf(t, d) = tf(t, d) \times idf(t, D).$$

TF-IDF gives greater importance to terms that occur multiple times in a small number of documents while downweighting terms that appear in multiple documents. It improves effectiveness by balancing recall (with term frequency) with precision (using inverse document frequency).

Word2Vec generates a dense vector representation of words, known as word embeddings. Unlike methods such as one-hot encoding that deliver sparse word vectors without any semantic information, *Word2Vec* maps each word to a continuous vector space. It relies on neighboring words to learn vectors for the target word and embeds semantic relationship between words into word vectors.

Word2Vec is a neural network-based method that captures the semantic relationship between words in such a way that words with similar meanings are located closer to one another in the vector space. Such vector representations are useful in tasks such as machine translation. *Word2Vec* uses distributed representations, based on the idea that words appearing in similar contexts will have similar meaning, and their representations will be closer in the vector space. When the words referring to similar contexts are projected in the same space then they appear closer to each other [4, 7].

There are two approaches to *Word2Vec*: *skip-gram* and *continuous bag of words (CBOW)*.

The objective of a *skip-gram* model is to predict the surrounding context words given a single target word. It begins with a naive representation (e.g. a one-hot encoding) and learns a dense, low dimensional embedding that can effectively predict nearby words. *Skip-gram* is well suited for large datasets, and has the advantage of learning high-quality representations for rare words, as it uses each occurrence of the target words to predict multiple neighboring context words. It maximizes the following likelihood:

$$\sum_{t=1}^{T} \sum_{c \in C_t} \log p(w_c | w_t).$$

Here, a word w_t is surrounded by words w_c in context C_t.

In *CBOW*, a context window containing terms appearing around a word in a document is used to represent that word. The target word appears in the middle of the context window. This approach is different from traditional approaches, where the algorithm predict the next word based on several preceding words. A neural network combines the representation of words from the window and predicts the target word. The words in the context window are treated as an unordered collection, and their combined representations are used to predict the missing word. *CBOW* can be trained on a large corpus and learns a representation of frequent words in the dataset.

Both architectures are implemented using a shallow, two-layer neural network. Words are taken as input and processed through a single hidden layer, and the output layer produces a probability distribution over the entire vocabulary. The model assigns scores to every word in the context, and this distribution is used to learn the embeddings. A softmax activation function is used over the output layer's scores (logits) to produce a probability distribution indicating the target word or context word. In the process of training with backpropagation and optimization for the task, the network adjusts its weights. The modified internal weights then become the context-aware word vectors [8].

For example, if a collection of words also contains a phrase 'fly me to moon', Fig. 4.1. In case of *CBOW* model, it removes the word 'me' from the context window and train a model to predict that the removed word correctly fills the blank. In case of

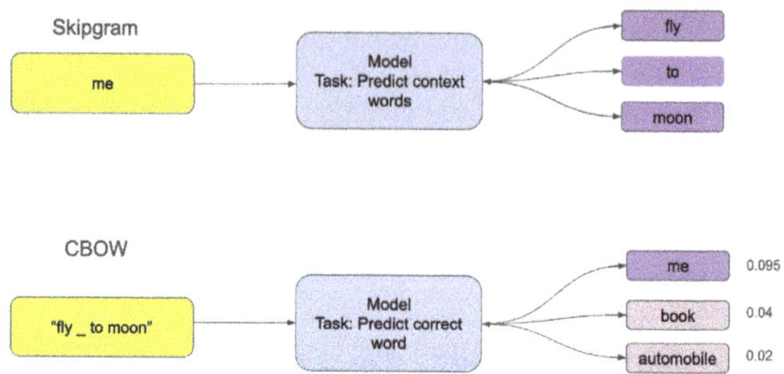

Fig. 4.1 *Word2Vec* Architecture. The *skip-gram* model takes the word 'me' as input and predicts probabilities over all words in the vocabulary. Consider the phrase *fly me to moon* that may appear multiple times in the corpus. The words 'fly', 'to' and 'moon' will tend to have higher than other predicted probabilities as context words of 'me', as compared to other words. During training, the model adjusts the embedding of 'me' so that its vector representation becomes closer to those of its frequent context words. Conversely, in the *CBOW* model, given the surrounding words in a phrase with one word removed, the model is trained to predict the missing word correctly

skip-gram, the model generates a set of embeddings for all words in the vocabulary. Using the word *me* as input, the model predicts several probabilities for the entire phrase [9].

GloVe. The Global Vectors model, or *GloVe*, encodes semantic as well as syntactic similarities in its word vectors [10] . Unlike the distributed representation approach used in *Word2Vec* models, which use local context, *GloVe*'s training objective is to learn information from the entire corpus. The main idea behind *GloVe* is that the starting point for vector learning should be the ratio of co-occurrence probabilities rather than raw co-occurrence probability scores. Their relationship is found by examining their co-occurrences with respect to various probe words, $\tilde{w}_k$. $P_{ij} = P(j|i) = \frac{X_{ij}}{X_i}$ represents the probability that word j occurs in the context of word i. X_i is the number of times any word occurs in the context of i, $X_i = \sum_k X_{ik}$, and X_{ij} is the count of the number of times word j occurs in the context of i. If word k is related to word i, then the ratio of P_{ik}/P_{jk} will be large, and if word k is related to j, then the ratio will be small. If k has very little relationship to either word then the ratio would be close to 1.

The *GloVe* model learns a dense vector representation based on semantic information, similarity between word vectors, and syntactical information (statistical ratio of co-occurrence probabilities) [10]. The cost function of the model can be written as:

$$J = \sum_{i,j=1}^{V} f(X_{ij})(w_i^T \tilde{w}_j + b_i + \tilde{b}_j - \log(X_{ij}))^2.$$

Here, w_i, w_j are the word and context vectors and X_{ij} is the number of times of word j appears in context of word i. $f(X_{ij})$ is a weighting function that moderates the contribution of each co-occurrence pair. It down weighs extremely common and rare pairs, ensuring that they don't dominate the learning process. By minimizing this objective, *GloVe* constructs a vector space that encodes both semantic and syntactic information about words.

FastText/Subword Information Skip-Gram. Bojanowski et al. proposed a variation on the *skip-gram* model in which a word is represented as a bag of character n-grams [11]. In the *skip-gram* model, the objective is to maximize the following log likelihood:

$$\sum_{t=1}^{T} \sum_{c \in C_t} \log p(w_c | w_t),$$

where a large corpus is represented as a sequence of words $w_1, w_2, \ldots, w_t$ and context C_t is the set of words surrounding the word w_t. The probability of the context word occurring in the context can be defined with a softmax:

$$p(w_c | w_t) = \frac{e^{s(w_t, w_c)}}{\sum_{j=1}^{W} e^{s(w_t, j)}}.$$

The *skip-gram* model is limited, as given a word w_t, it only predicts one context word w_c.

The *FastText* model uses a *skip-gram* model with negative sampling [11, 12]. It considers all context words as positive examples and sample random negative words from the corpus. The objective transforms into the following negative log-likelihood:

$$\log(1 + e^{-s(w_t, w_c)}) + \sum_{n \in N_{t,c}} \log(1 + e^{s(w_t, n)}),$$

where a set of negative words is represented by $N_{t,c}$. The score is computed as a scalar product between word and context vecotrs $s(w_t, w_c) = u_{w_t}^{T} v_{w_c}$. Vectors u_{w_t} and v_{w_c} are word vectors for words w_t and w_c.

The *skip-gram* model uses a distinct vector representation for for each word, and ignores information related to internal structure and formation of words. In contrast, the *fast-text* model learns a vector representation for each character n-gram and the word vector is represented as a sum of the n-gram vectors. The scoring function s finds the relationship between a target word and a context and can be written as $s(w_t, w_c) = \mathbf{u}_{w_t} \mathbf{v}_{w_c}$, where $\mathbf{u}_{w_t}, \mathbf{v}_{w_c}$ are the word vector representations for target word w_t and context word w_c, respectively. Each word is represented by an n-gram bag of characters, the word w is also included in the n-grams set. For example, for the word *hello* with $n = 3$, the character n-grams are: $< he, hel, ell, llo, lo >, < hello >$, where symbols $<, >$ are used to distinguish a sequence from other character sequences.

A word w_t is represented as G_{w_t}, the set of n-grams of w_t. The vector representation of the word is the sum of the vector representation of its n-grams.

ELMo. The *Embeddings from Language Models*, or *ELMo*, assigns a representation to each token as a function of the entire sentence [13]. *ELMo* uses bi-directional LSTMs (BiLM) along with a weighted combination of hidden states and an embedding layer to learn contextualized embeddings [14, 15]. A sentence l, is represented as a set of N tokens $t_1, t_2, \ldots, t_N$. Under a bidirectional language model (BiLM), a forward language model ($\overrightarrow{\theta_{LSTM}}$) predicts the probability of a sequence by modeling the probability of a current token based on preceding tokens; and similarly, a backward language model ($\overleftarrow{\theta_{LSTM}}$) runs the sequence in reverse order, predicting the previous token based on future context. They can be represented as:

$$p(t_1, t_2, \ldots, t_N) = \prod_{k=1}^{N} p(t_k | t_1, t_2, \ldots, t_{k-1}),$$

and

$$p(t_1, t_2, \ldots, t_N) = \prod_{k=1}^{N} p(t_k | t_{k+1}, t_{k+2}, \ldots, t_N).$$

The BiLM then maximizes the log-likelihood of both directions:

$$\sum_{k=1}^{N} (\log p(t_k | t_1, t_2, \ldots, t_{k-1}; \theta_X, \overrightarrow{\theta_{LSTM}}, \theta_s)$$

$$+ (\log t_k | t_{k+1}, t_{k+2}, \ldots, t_N; \theta_X, \overleftarrow{\theta_{LSTM}}, \theta_s)).$$

Parameters are shared for embedding (θ_X) and softmax layer (θ_s), and maintain separate parameters for LSTMs (θ_{LSTM}) in each direction. The *ELMo* vector representation for a word is sum of the weighted combination of initial word vectors, and concatenated hidden layers of both directions.

GPT. Leveraging a decoder-only transformer architecture [16, 17] Radford et al. proposed a *GPT* model that uses a larger corpus of varied training data on a multi-layer transformer-decoder language model to learn word representations [6]. This model uses a multi-headed self-attention operation over input tokens with a context window that leverages only preceding tokens to predict well the current token with an output distribution using a softmax layer.

It aims to maximize the following likelihood: $L_1(U) = \sum_i \log P(u_i | u_k, \ldots, u_{i-1}; \theta)$.

Here, $U = u_1, u_2, \ldots, u_n$ is the set of unsupervised tokens and P is modeled with a neural network with parameters θ. If W_e is the initial token embedding representation, then output distributions over target tokens can be learned as:

$$h_0 = U W_e + W_p,$$
$$h_l = transformer - block(h_{l-1}) \forall i \in [1, n], \tag{4.1}$$
$$P(u) = softmax(h_n W_e^T).$$

Here, U is the context number of tokens, n is the number of layers and W_p is the position encoding matrix.

BERT. Using the encoder transformer architecture [17], Devlin et al. proposed the *Bidirectional Encoder Representations from the Transformer* model, or *BERT* [5]. Similar to *ELMo* and unlike *GPT*, *BERT* leverages left and right context, but instead of separate LSTM features, it jointly conditions on both left and right contexts across all layers. It uses a masked language model approach where some percentage of the input tokens are masked at random. *BERT* masks 15% of all tokens in each sequence at random. The model's objective then is to predict the vocabulary IDs of the masked tokens while jointly conditioning on the left and right context using bidirectional self-attention.

4.3 Methods to Debias Word Embeddings

Even though various words embedding methods use significantly different approaches, they all use context windows– surrounding words– to transfer statistical relationships and semantic structure between words into dense numerical vectors.

Advances in word embeddings also raise a question regarding historical and cultural nuances contained within words. Text, as a form of language representation, is used to communicate and project human interactions, and possesses features that define a social world [18]. Text also shapes how past events, history and culture are documented and interpreted. Power dynamics, social discrimination, traditional and existing stereotypes also find their way into written words and into statistical and semantic relationship between words.

Stereotypical associations such as *men:doctors* and *women:nurses* easily find their way into word embeddings, as reported by Bolukabasi et al. [19]. Gender bias and sexism is also represented in word associations due to the long history of gender discrimination in professional spaces [20]. These are only a few of many examples to illustrate how biases can enter the information retrieval systems through word embedding vectors. Therefore, it is crucial to quantify and mitigate biases in word embeddings, as they are part of the initial steps in training IR systems, where collected data is converted into numerical vectors and enter into IR algorithmic pipeline.

A method to debias word embeddings is given by Bolukabasi et al. [19], as described in Sect. 3.2.2. This method identifies a *gender subspace* **g** with the help of defining sets of gender associative words $D_1, D_2, \ldots, D_n \subset W$, such as (*she, he*)(*woman, man*) (*girl,boy*). Then the mean vector of the set is defined as:

$$\mu_i = \sum_{w \in D_i} \mathbf{w}/|D_i|,$$

where $\mathbf{w}$ is the given word embedding. Singular value decomposition (SVD) is used to identify a bias subspace as

$$C := \sum_{i=1}^{n} \sum_{w \in D_i} (\mathbf{w} - \mu_i)^T (\mathbf{w} - \mu_i)/|D_i|.$$

The first k rows of C define a bias subspace B.

Given this subspace, there are two potential ways of debiasing the word embedding. *Neutralize and Equalize* (hard debiasing) and *Soften* (soft debiasing). *Neutralize* ensures that the neutral words, such as 'doctor', have zero component in the gender direction. *Equalize* makes sure that a neutral word, such as *babysit*, is equidistant to the word pairs in the equality set, such as (*grandmother, grandfather*) (*gal, guy*). Here, the word *babysit* is equidistant to both equalize pairs but closer to *grandmother* and *grandfather*. In the case of *Equalize*, semantic distinctions that are useful in applications may be removed. For instance, one would expect the phrase 'a gentleman's club' to have a much higher probability than 'a gentlelady's club', because although *gentlelady* is grammatically correct, the latter phrase is rarely used in practice. However, if the embeddings of *gentleman* and *gentlelady* are forced into symmetry, their phrase embeddings may be treated as equally plausible, thereby erasing a meaningful semantic relationship encoded in the vectors.

The *Soften* algorithm attempts to reduce the difference between such word pairs, while retaining as much similarity to the original embeddings as possible.

4.3.1 Hard and Soft Debiasing

Hard debiasing. For gender-neutral words, one can remove the part of the vector that lies on the gender subspace. If $N \in W$ are the words to neutralize, then for each word $w \in N$ one can re-embed it as $\mathbf{w} = (\mathbf{w} - \mathbf{w_B})/||\mathbf{w} - \mathbf{w_B}||$. For the words in the equality set, such as *grandmother, grandfather*, vectors such as *babysit* should still retain some gender information, but they should be equidistant from the gender-bias axis.

To accomplish this, for each word $E \in \mathcal{E}$, where $\mathcal{E}$ is the set of equalized words, first find the average embedding $\mu := \sum_{w \in E} w/|E|$, and then project it on the bias subspace as $v := \mu - \mu_B$, where μ_B is the projection of μ onto the bias subspace. If B is the gender subspace in embedding w, then $\mu_B = \sum_{j=1}^{k} (\mu \cdot b_j) b_j$. Here, subspace B is defined by k orthogonal unit vectors. Finally, for each word $w \in E$, we have:

$$\mathbf{w} = v + \sqrt{1 - ||v||^2} \frac{\mathbf{w_b} - \mu_B}{||\mathbf{w_B} - \mu_B||}.$$

Here, the vectors in the equalized set become equal in their bias-neutral component and are symmetrically arranged in their bias directions. This ensures that for any gender neutral word w and any equalized pair words e_1, e_2, $\mathbf{w} \cdot \mathbf{e_1} = \mathbf{w} \cdot \mathbf{e_2}$ and $||\mathbf{w} - \mathbf{e_1}|| = ||\mathbf{w} - \mathbf{e_2}||$.

Soft bias correction. Soft-bias correction is a relaxed procedure that aims to preserve the semantic structure of the embedding while reducing gender bias and minimizing the projection of gender-neutral words onto the gender subspace. It is defined as

$$min_T ||(TW)^T (TW) - W^T W||_F^2 + \lambda ||(TN)^T (TB)||_F^2.$$

Here, the first term of the objective preserves the geometry of embedding space, the second term minimizes bias from neutral words, λ is a tuning parameter, and T is the desired debiasing transformation $T \in \mathbb{R}^{d \times d}$. The normalized unit length, less the biased output embedding can be retrieved as $\hat{\mathbf{W}}_{new} = Tw/||Tw||_2, w \in W$.

4.3.2 Gender Neutral Word Embeddings

is another gender-neutral word embedding method that preserves gender information in some attributes while neutralizing gender influence from other dimensions [21]. A word vector w consists of two parts $w = [w_a, w_g]$, standing for neutralized and gendered components, respectively. The minimization objective is defined as $J = J_G + \lambda_d J_D + \lambda_e J_E$. Here, J_G is the objective from the *GloVe* word embedding model and λ_d, λ_e are hyperparameters [10]. Given a set of pair of association seed words (W_M, W_F), J_D can be defined as:

$$J_D^{L_1} = -|| \sum_{w \in W_M} w^g - \sum_{w \in W_F} w^g ||_1. \tag{4.2}$$

This approach minimizes the negative distances between male and female seed words.

J_D can also be defined in terms of the L2 norm:

$$J_D^{L_2} = \sum_{w \in W_M} ||\beta_1 \mathbf{e} - w^g||_2^2 + \sum_{w \in W_F} ||\beta_2 \mathbf{e} - w^g||_2^2. \tag{4.3}$$

Here, $\mathbf{e}$ is a vector of all ones, with the same dimensions as w^g. $[\beta_1, \beta_2]$ can have arbitrary values (they are set to $[1, -1]$ respectively, in [21]). This vector forces the male words w^g vectors to move towards β_1 while moving female word w^g vectors to move towards β_2, increasing the separation between groups along the gender direction.

The third component of the objective function J_E ensures that the neutral word vectors are orthogonal to the gender direction $\mathbf{v_g}$. One can calculate the gender direction vector as:

$$v_g = \frac{1}{|\Omega'|} \sum_{(w_m, w_f) \in \Omega'} (w_m^{(a)} - w_f^{(a)}).$$

Here, Ω' is the set of predefined gender word pairs. v_g is the average of difference of male and female word vectors for words in set Ω'.

We then have

$$J_E = \sum_{w \in \Omega_N} (v_g^T w^a)^2.$$

Here Ω_N is the set of neutral words. The loss ensures that non-gender attributes of neutral words have no alignment with the gender direction of the embedding.

4.3.3 Bias Mitigation in Gendered Languages Word Embeddings

In case of gendered languages that contain sex-dependent words, as discussed in Sect. 3.2.4, one can use dualities such as *good,bad, love,hate, happy,sad,* and so on to find a sentiment direction. Similar to methodology used by Bolukbasi et al. to find the gender subspace, the sentiment direction **s** is obtained by applying PCA on the difference of the word vector pairs in the duality list. Given a list of neutral words $N = \mathbf{w_1}, \mathbf{w_2}, \ldots, \mathbf{w_n}$, hard debiasing is performed as:

$$\mathbf{w_i'} = \mathbf{w_i} - \frac{\mathbf{w_i} \cdot \mathbf{s}}{\mathbf{s} \cdot \mathbf{s}} \mathbf{s},$$

where $\mathbf{w_i'}$ is the debiased non normalized vector for word w_i Here, vectors of the neutral words are orthogonal to the sentiment vector. This method mitigates the bias at the word embeddings level. Another debiasing method proposed in the paper, uses a support vector machine to learn a hyperplane defined by a vector **p**. This vector corresponds to the sentiment direction obtained at the word embedding space. The neutral words are hard-neutralize ensuring that they have no component in the sentiment direction [18].

References

1. Blei DM, Ng AY, Jordan MI (2003) Latent dirichlet allocation. J Mach Learn Res 3(null):993–1022
2. Jones KS (1986) Synonymy and semantic classification, Edinburgh information technology series. Edinburgh University Press,
3. Landauer TK, Foltz PW, Laham D (1998) An introduction to latent semantic analysis. Discourse Proc 25(2–3):259–284
4. Mikolov T, Chen K, Corrado GS, Dean J (2013) Efficient estimation of word representations in vector space. In: International conference on learning representations
5. Devlin J, Chang M-W, Lee K, Toutanova K (2019) BERT: pre-training of Deep Bidirectional Transformers for Language Understanding. In: Burstein J, Doran C, Solorio T (eds) Proceedings of the 2019 conference of the North American chapter of the association for computational linguistics: human language technologies, Volume 1 (Long and Short Papers), Minneapolis, Minnesota, pp 4171–4186. Association for Computational Linguistics
6. Radford A (2011) Improving language understanding with unsupervised learning. OpenAI Res

7. Mikolov T, Le QV, Sutskever I (2013) Exploiting similarities among languages for machine translation. ArXiv preprint arXiv 1309:4168

8. Goldberg Y, Levy O (2014) word2vec explained: deriving mikolov et al.'s negative-sampling word-embedding method. CoRR, abs/1402.3722

9. Boykis V (2023) What are embeddings?

10. Pennington J, Socher R, Manning CD (2014) GloVe: global vectors for word representation. In: Empirical Methods in natural language processing (EMNLP), pp 1532–1543

11. Bojanowski P, Grave E, Joulin A, Mikolov T (2017) Enriching word vectors with subword information. Trans Assoc Comput Linguist 5:135–146

12. Mikolov T, Sutskever I, Chen K, Corrado G, Dean J (2013) Distributed representations of words and phrases and their compositionality. In: Proceedings of the 27th international conference on neural information processing systems—Volume 2, NIPS'13, Red Hook, NY, USA, pp 3111–3119 Curran Associates Inc

13. Peters ME, Neumann M, Iyyer M, Gardner M, Clark C, Lee K, Zettlemoyer L (2018) Deep contextualized word representations. In: Walker M, Ji H, Stent A (eds) Proceedings of the 2018 conference of the North American chapter of the association for computational linguistics: human language technologies, Volume 1 (Long Papers). New Orleans, Louisiana, pp 2227–2237. Association for Computational Linguistics

14. Graves A, Fernández S, Schmidhuber J (2005) Bidirectional LSTM networks for improved phoneme classification and recognition. In: Duch W, Kacprzyk J, Oja E, Zadrożny S (eds) Artificial neural networks: formal models and their applications–ICANN 2005, Berlin, Heidelberg. Springer, Berlin Heidelberg, pp 799–804

15. Hochreiter S, Schmidhuber J (1997) Long short-term memory. Neural Comput 9(8):1735–1780

16. Liu PJ, Saleh M, Pot E, Goodrich B, Sepassi R, Kaiser L, Shazeer N (2018) Generating wikipedia by summarizing long sequences. In: International conference on learning representations

17. Vaswani A, Shazeer N, Parmar N, Uszkoreit J, Jones L, Gomez AN, Kaiser Ł, Polosukhin I (2017) Attention is all you need. In: Proceedings of the 31st international conference on neural information processing systems, NIPS'17, Red Hook, NY, USA, pp 6000–6010. Curran Associates Inc

18. Papakyriakopoulos O, Hegelich S, Serrano JCM, Marco F (2020) Bias in word embeddings. In: Proceedings of the 2020 conference on fairness, accountability, and transparency, FAT* '20, New York, NY, USA, pp 446–457. Association for Computing Machinery

19. Bolukbasi T, Chang K-W, Zou J, Saligrama V, Kalai A (2016) Man is to computer programmer as woman is to Homemaker? Debiasing Word Embeddings. In: Proceedings of the 30th international conference on neural information processing systems, NIPS'16, Red Hook, NY, USA, pp 4356–4364. Curran Associates Inc

20. Ross K, Carter C (2011) Women and news: a long and winding road. Media Culture & Society 33(8):1148–1165

21. Zhao J, Zhou Y, Li Z, Wang W, Chang K-W (2018) Learning gender-neutral word embeddings. In: Riloff E, Chiang D, Hockenmaier J, Tsujii J (eds) Proceedings of the 2018 conference on empirical methods in natural language processing Brussels, Belgium, pp 4847–4853. Association for Computational Linguistics

Chapter 5
Fair Information Retrieval Methods

Abstract In this chapter, we discuss techniques to reduce bias in the display of search results, including methods for re-ranking results or suggesting alternative queries. We begin with a discussion of fairness principles that apply to these tasks, and then present several fair ranking algorithms. We conclude the chapter with a discussion of balanced query recommendation, the goal of which is to recommend alternative search queries that maintain high relevance but provide more balanced representation of various groups.

5.1 Introduction

Information Retrieval (IR) plays a critical role in obtaining relevant results for a user's information need. Results may be ranked, rated, or selected based on an IR application, such as recommendation platforms, search engines, etc. However, it is important to note that IR systems can reflect or even amplify existing biases [1, 2]. One possible explanation for the biased behavior of IR systems is that the output of IR systems heavily depends on the data that they have access to. If the datasets contain historic or existing societal biases, then the systems end up learning from them. The results from these systems can reflect or even amplify such biases (see Chaps. 2 and 3).

There are two definitions of fairness that may be taken into consideration for IR systems. 1) *Group fairness* states that group demographics in the output of a machine learning system should be proportional to the demographic values in the population. 2) *Individual fairness* refers to a principle that any two items that are similar with respect to a task should be treated similarly [3].

Along with the fairness definitions, we must also pay attention to how biases can enter a IR setup. Zehlike et al. define two main intervention points for bias mitigation efforts in IR models: pre-processing methods that work on learning fair representations of data; and in-processing and post-processing methods that utilize a learning objective to deliver fair results as output [4].

© The Author(s), under exclusive license to Springer Nature Switzerland AG 2026   61
H. Mishra and S. Soundarajan, *Addressing Bias in Information Retrieval*,
SpringerBriefs in Intelligent Systems, https://doi.org/10.1007/978-3-032-24145-0_5

In the next section, we discuss various pre-, in-, and post-processing algorithms that mitigate biases by ranking and re-ranking results based on definitions of individual and group fairness.

5.2 Fair Ranking Algorithms

Fair ranking algorithms ensure individual fairness and fair group representations by direct interventions on the ordering of ranked outputs. Typically, these methods either re-rank results to deliver fair outputs, or learn fair representations for data points to minimize the impact of sensitive attributes in algorithmic decisions.

iFair [5]. Based on the individual fairness objective [3], this method learns a fair representations of data points. Consider two candidates who have almost identical resumes. A system should deliver similar judgments for the two candidates, setting aside possible biases that can be induced into the algorithmic framework due to the presence of sensitive attributes such as gender, race, or ethnicity [5].

iFair transforms an input data point X_a, the feature vector for candidate a, into an output representation $\tilde{X}_a$, using a mapping ϕ. Two individuals (a,b) that are similar with respect to their non-protected attributes X/A (where A represent sensitive attributes) should also be indistinguishable in their fair representations $\phi(X_a)$, where sensitive attributes are included.

$$|d(\phi(X_a), \phi(X_b)) - d(X_a^*, X_b^*)| \leq \epsilon.$$

Here, X_a^* represents the non-protected features of a, and $\phi(X_a)$ represents the fair transformation of features of candidate a. Distance measure d is used to find distances between two candidates in the original feature space and, in the transformed space. Lahoti et al. [5] used Minkowski p-metrics for the distance measures:

$$d(X_a, X_b) = [\sum_{n=1}^{N} \alpha_n (x_{a,n} - X_{b,n})^p]^{1/p}.$$

Here, α is an $N-$dimensional vector for tunable weights for different attributes.

The transformation $\phi(X_a)$ is formalized as a soft-clustering or probabilistic clustering problem that, given K clusters, each represented by a vector v_k and a probability distribution vector P_a, assigns candidate x_a to one of the clusters. The probability vector P_a for candidate x_a is:

$$P_{ak} = \frac{exp(-d(x_a, v_k))}{\sum_{j=1}^{K} exp(-d(x_a, v_j))},$$

and the mapping ϕ that transforms x_i into $\tilde{x}_i$ is:

$$\phi(X_a) = \tilde{X}_a = \sum_{k=1..K} P_{ak} \cdot v_k.$$

The *iFair* algorithm uses two utility objectives, reconstruction loss and a fair objective to make sure learned representations preserve pair-wise distances between candidates on non-protected attributes.

The reconstruction loss between X and $\tilde{X}$ is defined as:

$$L_{util}(X, \tilde{X}) = \sum_{i=1}^{M} ||x_i - \tilde{x}_i||_2.$$

The fairness loss ensures that items maintain pair-wise distances in original (non-protected attributes) and transformed representations:

$$L_{fair}(X, \tilde{X}) = \sum_{i,j=1...M} (d(\phi(x_i), \phi(x_j)) - d(x_i^*, x_j^*))^2.$$

The loss objective utilizes the reconstruction and fair loss as:

$$L = \lambda \cdot L_{util}(X, \tilde{X}) + \mu \cdot L_{fair}(X, \tilde{X}),$$

where λ and μ are hyper-parameters and L is optimized using gradient descent.

Algorithm FA*IR [6]. This algorithm focuses on group fairness [3]. It uses a target distribution $\hat{p}$, which can either be derived from population demographics or configured specifically for a task. At every prefix of the ranking, it compares the number of protected elements seen so far with the expected number of protected elements if they were picked randomly using Bernoulli trials [6] (see Section 3.3.2).

It uses two priority queues for two separate groups, where one queue is for the target protected group. There are k items each in both queues. For each position in the ranking, it computes the minimum number of protected candidates needed, guided by item attributes, group alignments, and relevance scores. If the algorithm decides that it needs a protected candidate at a position, then the best item is pulled from its queue.

The running time for the FA^*IR algorithm is $O(n + k \log k)$. It takes $O(n)$ time to iterate through n items and $O(k \log k)$ time to build and sort the two priority queues of size $O(k)$. If the two lists are already available, then the running time reduces to $O(k \log k)$.

Fairness-Aware Ranking at LinkedIn [7]. In this work, the desired fairness properties of the ranking are defined through the minimum and maximum number of candidates at each position in a ranking list. Geyik et al. proposed following ranked list constraints:

$$\forall k \leq |\tau_r|, \forall a_i \in A, count_k(a_i) \leq \lceil p_{a_i} \cdot k \rceil \quad \text{and}$$

$$\forall k \leq |\tau_r|, \forall a_i \in A, count_k(a_i) \geq \lfloor p_{a_i} \cdot k \rfloor.$$

k is used to define top-k results in the ranked list τ_r returned in response to a request r, A is a set of disjoint protected attribute values: $A = a_1, a_2, \ldots, a_l$, where each candidate has exactly one value in A, a_i is the $i_t h$ attribute value, and p_{a_i} is the desired proportion of candidates in tau_r with value a_i.

The algorithm, through the first inequality, checks if any group is yet to meet the minimum number of requirements. If so, then the candidate from that group is added to the ranking. If the minimum conditions are met, the algorithm selects the candidate with the highest score from groups that have not yet exceeded the maximum count [4, 7]. The authors propose three fair ranking algorithms:

1. *DetGreedy*: At each step, if some attribute value's minimum representation constraint is at risk of being violated, select the highest-scoring candidate from among those with that attribute. Otherwise, select the next highest-scoring candidate whose inclusion will not cause its attribute value to exceed the maximum representation constraint.

2. *DetCons* and *DetRelaxed*: Similar to *DetGreedy*, if there are any attribute values for which the minimum number constraint is about to be violated, the method select the candidate with the highest score among them. Otherwise, for the attribute values that are yet to meet the maximum number requirement, it favors the attribute values for which the minimum number requirement is soon to be violated in the ranking. In *DetCons*, the algorithm select the attribute value minimizing $\frac{\lceil p_{a_i} \cdot k \rceil}{p_{a_i}}$ and in *DetRelaxed*, it considers all attribute values that minimize $\lceil \frac{\lceil p_{a_i} \cdot k \rceil}{p_{a_i}} \rceil$ and select the candidate with highesr score among them.

3. *DetConstSort*: Unlike the previous greedy algorithm, *DetConstSort* waits for multiple indices of recommendation before deciding on the next candidate and the attribute value. It aims to satisfy the quality of the ranked list, subject to constraints that some candidates can not go beyond a specific index [7].

DELTR: Disparate Exposure in Learning to Rank [8], considers items belonging to two separate groups, denoted by G^+ and G^-, where G^+ is the target protected group. Due to historical or existing biases, a ranked list may result in disproportionate exposure to privileged groups. The method minimizes unfairness in terms of disparities in exposure of items represented by average exposure of groups (see Section 3.3.4). A query q is associated with a list of documents $d^q \in D$, and each document is represented by a feature vector $x_i^{(q)}$. Zehlike et al. define exposure of a document using probabilistic ranking P as:

$$Exposure(x_i^{(q)}|P_{\hat{y}^{(q)}}) = P_{\hat{y}^{(q)}}(x_i^q) \cdot v_1,$$

where v_1 is the position bias of position 1, indicating the relative importance of document d in a ranking system. The average exposure of documents associated with a group G^p is defined as:

$$Exposure(G^p | P_{\hat{y}^{(q)}}) = \frac{1}{G^p} \sum Exposure(x_i^{(q)} | P_{\hat{y}^{(q)}}).$$

Using the principle of demographic parity, ensuring equal exposure to items across different groups, a new unfairness criteria is introduced:

$$D(\hat{Y}) = \max(0, Exposure(G^- | P_{\hat{y}^{(q)}}) - Exposure(G^+ | P_{\hat{y}^{(q)}}))^2.$$

The squared hinge loss only detects unfairness if the protected group receives less exposure than the other group [8].

The algorithm *DELTR* incorporates the unfairness metric $D(\hat{Y})$ and a relevance measure L into its objective function as:

$$L_{DELTR}(Y, \hat{Y}) = L(Y, \hat{Y}) + \gamma D(\hat{Y}).$$

Gradient descent is used to solved the optimization problem [4, 8].

Rankings With Equity of Attention [9]. The discussion on exposure in fair rankings in the preceding section has a counterpart in the discussion around equity of amortized attention. Given a sequence of rankings, each item should receive cumulative attention proportional to their cumulative relevance [9].

Biega et al. measure unfairness based on the L1-norm of attention and relevance received by items in a sequence of rankings (see Section 3.3.5 for discussion on Equity of Amortized Attention metric):

$$unfairness(l^1, l^2, \ldots, l^m) = \sum_{i=1}^{n} |A_i - R_i| = \sum_{i=1}^{n} \left| \sum_{j=1}^{m} a_i^j - \sum_{j=1}^{m} r_i^j \right|,$$

where $l^1, l^2, \ldots, l^m$ are a sequence of rankings extracted for a query q, a_i^j is the attention value of item u_i in ranking l^j, and, similarly, r_i^j is the relevance of the item u_i in ranking l^j and $\{u_1, u_2, \ldots, u_n\}$ are the set of items to be ranked.

In order to satisfy a fairness criterion, less-relevant items are ranked higher. The permuted 'fair' rankings can lead to quality loss in the relevance of the ranked list. One can use Normalized discounted cumulative gain (NDCG) to measure the quality of a permuted list. If l is the original ranking and l^* is the permuted ranked list then the ratio of $DCG@k(l^*)$ to $DCG@k(l)$ gives us the quality of the permuted list. There are other metrics such as Kendall's Tau or MAP-quality that can be used as well.

Discounted cumulative gain (DCG) measures the quality of the ranking by assigning higher weight to items at the top and logarithmically discounting items at lower positions:

$$DCG@k(r) = \sum_{i=1}^{k} \frac{2^{r(i)} - 1}{\log_2(i + 1)},$$

where $r(i)$ is the relevance score of item at position i in the ranking.

Offline Optimization. Suppose that rankings $l^1, l^2, \ldots, l^m$ are available and one wishes to reorder them to $l^{1*}, l^{2*}, \ldots, l^{m*}$. The method minimizes the absolute difference between cumulative attention and cumulative relevance for item u_i.

$$minimize \sum_i |A_i - R_i|,$$

$$\text{subject to } NDCG - quality@k(l, l^*) \geq \theta, j = 1, \ldots, m,$$

where A_i and R_i are, respectively, the cumulated attention and relevance scores for item u_i across m rankings.

Online Optimization. In an online setting, queries are not assumed to be available beforehand, and the system receives one query at a time. For ranking in such an online setting, Biega et al. permute the rankings based on cumulated attention and relevance scores distributions seen in the previous rankings.

$$minimize \sum_i |A_i^{m-1} + a_i^m - (R_i^{m-1} + r_i^m)|,$$

$$\text{subject to } NDCG - quality@k(l, l^*) \geq \theta.$$

Here, A_i^{l-1} and R_i^{l-1} are cumulated attention and relevance scores that item u_i has received up to and including ranking l^{m-1}.

5.3 Background: Multi-stage Ranking

Information Retrieval (IR) is a process of finding a set of relevant items from a collection based on an information need. Web-based search engines, for example, return a ranked list of results in response to a user's query. A key challenge in this process is position bias, where items at the top receive significantly more engagement than the lower-ranked items. For efficient retrieval, items ranked in the top positions must be relevant to the user's query. Methods such as multi-stage ranking have been proposed for improved retrieval of results [10]. Multi-stage ranking breaks the process into multiple stages. Each stage ranks the given documents and passes a top-k set of documents to the next stage, until the final set of results is returned to the user. Earlier machine learning based methods were based on manual feature engineering processes [11]. The introduction of deep learning methods provided an advanced way to rank a list of documents. Using vector representations for queries and the documents, and deep learning methods such as convolutional neural networks and recurrent neural networks, captured more semantic relationships between the query and document vectors, delivering a higher relevance score for more relevant documents [12, 13].

Recent re-ranking approaches use pretrained contextual representation models such as *ELMo* and *BERT* [14, 15]. These are Bidirectional models that utilize both left-to-right and right-to-left contexts. Such as the word 'bank' present in two sentences, 'go to the *bank* and deposit money', and 'the river *bank* seems depleted' will be assigned two different vector representations based on the context. This is a different approach than assigning a single representation to a word, irrespective of the context, as done by models such as *Word2Vec* and *GloVe* [16, 17]. The contextual information present in the *ELMo* and *BERT* vector representations, along with IR models, is used to deliver improved ranked retrieval.

Multi-stage Document Ranking with BERT [18]. Nogueira et al. proposed a multi-stage ranking architecture, where the first stage h_0 retrieves results using a traditional inverted index model such as *BM25* [19–21]. Each later stage receives a top-k list of documents from the previous stage; each stage in turn provides a re-ranked list of documents to the next stage. The proposed architecture uses a *BM25* retrieval in the first stage h_0, followed by a *monoBERT* h_1 and *duoBERT* h_2 retrieval. The final ranked list of documents received from the *duoBERT* is returned to the user.

monoBERT. Given a query q, and a document d_i *monoBERT* passes the segment (query, document) through the *BERT* model, using [CLS] vector as input to a single-layer neural network, and a probability s_i is obtained, which signifies how much document d_i is relevant to query q. In the *BERT* architecture, [CLS] vector encodes semantic information about the given sentence segments (query and document, in this case). Based on probabilities s_i, the available candidates are re-ranked and a new list of candidate documents is generated, R_1, and used by the next stage of the pipeline. As defined in the work, the *monoBERT* model is trained using the following loss function:

$$L_{mono} = -\sum_{j \in J_{pos}} \log(s_j) - \sum_{j \in J_{neg}} \log(1 - s_j),$$

here J_{pos} is the set of relevant documents and J_{neg} is the set of non-relevant candidates in R_0. Datasets such as MS MARCO provide human-based judgments on relevant and non-relevant documents for a set of documents and queries [22, 23].

duoBERT. Using a pairwise approach, given a query q, a document d_i, another document d_j, and an implementation similar to *monoBERT*, using the [CLS] vector, a pairwise score p_{ij} is obtained. If there are k documents then a total of $k(k - 1)$ probabilities are computed. The *duoBERT* model is trained using the following loss function:

$$L_{duo} = -\sum_{i \in J_{pos}, j \in J_{neg}} \log(p_{i,j}) - \sum_{i \in J_{pos}, j \in J_{neg}} \log(1 - p_{i,j}).$$

The pairwise score $p_{i,j}$ is aggregated using methods such as sum, min, max, etc.

$$SUM : s_i = \sum_{j \in J_i} p_{i,j}; \quad MIN : s_i = \min_{j \in J_i} p_{i,j}; \quad MAX : s_i = \max_{j \in J_i} p_{i,j}$$

The aggregated score, s_i, assigns a single score to each document.

The final re-ranked list of documents R_2 obtained from *duoBERT*, using scores s_i, is returned to the user.

ColBERT [24]. In the method discussed above, the given query and a document form a sequence, which is then passed through the model to obtain scores. Khattab and Zaharia proposed an end-to-end ranking and a re-ranking method, *ColBERT*, based on a so-called *late interaction* mechanism between query and documents. In *ColBERT*, the query q and a document d are encoded through separate BERT-based encoders to obtain representations E_q and E_d. The relevance score between E_q and E_d is obtained through a process termed *late interaction*: For each term in the query $v \in q$, maximum cosine similarity is computed with vectors in E_d, and the outputs are combined via summation to obtain a relevance score between q and d. Similar to other re-rankers, given a query and a set of results returned by a term-based model such as *BM25*, one can apply *ColBERT* to re-rank the results and obtain a final top-k ranked list of results.

5.4 Adaptive Re-ranking

In an IR pipeline, an inexpensive model such as *BM25* is used for high recall by retrieving a large set of items [25]. Then, a re-ranker, maybe a deep learning based neural ranking model are used for higher precision, they re-score each item in the retrieved list, hopefully increasing utility by delivering a new and more relevant ranking to the user [26].

The capability of a re-ranker model is severely limited by the relevant documents that are retrieved during the first stage of retrieval. For example, if the majority of documents belonging to one group were not returned in the first stage of retrieval, then the final list of results returned by a re-ranker model will also be imbalanced.

MacAvaney et al. proposed *Graph-based Adaptive Re-ranking (GAR)*, an adaptive re-ranker that extends the capability of a standard re-ranking engine by including a set of documents that were not retrieved in the first round [27]. *GAR* is a graph-based re-ranking model that utilizes a corpus graph to find similar documents for each document returned in the first stage of retrieval. It then uses an alternative process to sample and re-rank a batch of documents. A new set of documents is retrieved using the corpus graph and added to a frontier set. Once it has explored the maximum number of documents that can be explored, it returns the final set of ranked list R as the output.

GAR can be used for fair re-ranking purposes as well, by ensuring the corpus graph is designed in a way to link documents with diverse groups. That is, if a document d with label A is retrieved in the first stage, then during the *GAR* extension process, when fetching similar documents for d, A fair *GAR* method only considers documents with labels other than A.

Jaenich et al. proposed adaptive re-ranking policies for fairness-aware exposure by leveraging the *GAR* re-ranking methodology [28]. They introduced four policies to consider, while adding documents after the first stage of retrieval. First, *removing neighbors from the same group*: After identifying all neighbors of a document d_i, they remove the neighbors that have the same group as the document d_i. This diversity is increased by giving exposure to documents from different groups. Second, *equal proportions among neighbors*: the policy places a quota on how many documents from different groups can be added. Third, *select high scoring documents from each group*: If documents from one group continue to rank higher and get more exposure than documents from other groups, then a bias is created. To counter this, instead of selecting the highest-ranked documents, one can select a set of high-scoring documents from each group. Fourth, *prioritize neighbors from the first iterations*: In this policy, instead of selecting high-scoring documents from every group, the policy selects the documents based on the order in which they were added to the frontier set.

Jaenich et al. used *BM25* as an initial ranker, and *monoT5* and *BERT-ELECTRA* as neural re-rankers [28–30]. For evaluation, they used *AWRF* metric [31]. They observed that *GAR* policies made the re-ranked list unfair compared to the baselines, which can be explained as *GAR* was developed to optimize for relevance only. The new re-ranking policies for fairness-aware exposure were able to distribute the exposure more fairly in the final re-ranked lists while maintaining the retrieval quality of the IR system [28].

5.5 Dynamic Learning-to-Rank

A dynamic *Learning-to-Rank (LTR)* method dynamically adapts its ranking policy based on user feedback. Platforms such as e-commerce or news sites consider user feedback while ranking items higher or lower based on clicks or other feedback received on items.

Given an information need, the system uses a ranking policy π_t and returns a set of results. The system presents the result to the user and receives feedback for every item in the result set. This feedback can be as simple as a 1 if the user engaged with the item and 0 otherwise. A dynamic *LTR* algorithm considers the feedback and produces a new ranking policy π_{t+1}, which is used the next time an information request is received.

Dynamic *LTR* suffers from a major drawback in that meaningful feedback is only received for items that a user interacts with. This leads to a rich-get-richer dynamic where top-ranked items receive more engagement than lower-ranked items, and the feedback updates the ranking policy in favor of top-ranked items. Another challenge faced by dynamic *LTR* is that the items belonging to certain groups may receive more feedback/ exposure than items from other groups. This can motivate the ranking policy to favor items from specific groups.

FairCo [32]. Morik et al. proposed *FairCo*, a proportional controller-based method that applies feedback into the ranking mechanism, proportional to the disparity in amortized fairness. Amortized fairness is measured by the absolute difference in how two groups are treated. This is calculated by comparing the ratio of exposure to utility for one group against the same ratio for the other group. It evaluates whether one group receives a disproportionate amount of exposure relative to the utility they provide, compared to a different group. (Also see the discussion on amortized fairness in Section:3.3.5). The larger disparity in amortized fairness highlights unfairness in the rankings. The *FairCo* ranking policy uses a combination of relevance scores and an error term. The error term represents the disparity value, which pushes items from less exposed groups upwards in the ranking.

5.6   Query Recommendation

Query reformulation methods such as query expansion, query refinement, query recommendation can lead to improved retrieval by adding semantically related terms to the original query, improving the quality of retrieved documents for a given information need.

Query refinement can occur through user interaction, where users may manually modify the query until satisfactory documents are retrieved, or through automatic query expansion approaches that improve the query at the system side.

Mishra and Soundarajan proposed a framework to recommend new queries that are related to the user's original queries, but whose search results contain less or opposing bias than the original query. The framework does not perform the search itself but leverages an existing search engine to curate results for the original and suggested queries [33].

We use notations as described in Table 3.1, where user's original query is denoted by q, D is a set of documents in the corpus, S is a given information retrieval system. A set of results returned for a query q is denoted by L. The method uses binomial group representation, with a document being either in a set of group G^+ or the group G^-.

5.6.1   Problem Setup

For the user's original query q, a search engine S performs a search on a corpus of documents D as $S(q, D)$ and returns a set of top-k results L. For each document d in L, the method collects metrics such as precision, recall, and F1-scores. F1-scores are used as the relevance scores, as true relevance of the document d to user u is not known beforehand. The method computes group membership information about each document (G^+, G^-) and create an average group membership (G) for L. Each document is assumed to be a part of only one group; defined as $G^+ = 1$ and $G^- = -1$. Thus G is an average of the biases of the individual documents in L.

5.6.2 Recommendation Framework: BQR

BalancedQR performs the following steps:

1. Given query q, a search system S, corpus of documents D, *BalancedQR* fetches $L_q = S(q, D)$, the top-k most relevant documents retrieved from D for q.
2. *BalancedQR* then calculates $relevance_q$ and G_q metrics. Here, relevance is the f1-score and G_q is average bias of L_q.
3. *BalancedQR* uses a word embedding and a large language model to create a set of candidate queries $q_1, q_2, \ldots, q_m$.
4. For each candidate query $q_1, q_2, \ldots, q_m$ and original query q, the method retrieves a set of search results and measures $relevance_{q_i}$ and G_{q_i}.
5. It is then treated as an multi-objective optimization problem, with relevance and bias as our two dimensions. *BalancedQR* finds the most optimal non-dominated set *recs* of queries. A query is non-dominated if there is no other query whose search results have both a lower bias and a higher relevance score.

The end user needs to be aware of word embeddings and the type of LLMs being used to generate candidate queries. The embeddings and the LLMs may contain biases themselves (see Chap. 4). *BalancedQR* is not inherently tied to any particular word embedding or LLM, and if less biased or unbiased word embeddings/LLMs are created, they can easily be used.

5.6.3 BQR: Results and Discussion

A sample result based on data collected from r/AskMen and r/AskWomen subreddits shows the *BalancedQR* analysis for the original and generated queries [33]. Using a *TF-IDF*-based search algorithm, *GloVe* word embedding (see Chap. 4) and a large language model, *BalancedQR* presents queries that deliver less biased search results than the results from the original query. Each document is assigned a score of +1 or -1, depending on whether they are a member of the *r/AskMen* or *r/AskWomen* subreddit, respectively.

Results for the original query 'loneliness' are shown in Fig. 5.1. Other candidate queries on the plot are generated by *GloVe* word embedding. The y-axis on the plot represents the 'relevance' metric; each relevance score is calculated as a *f1-score* based on search results from the original query and the candidate query. The x-axis on the plot represents bias score, which is the aggregated sum of bias of each document (each document is assigned a bias score of +1 or -1, based on its group membership) in the search results of the query, divided by the total number of search results for that query. If a query has more results from the *r/AskMen* subreddit, then it will be positioned on the right side of the plot, and on the left side if they have more results from the *r/AskWomen* subreddit.

The original query 'loneliness' returns results that are disproportionately from the *r/AskMen* subreddit. Similarly, candidate queries such as *anguish* and *grief* also

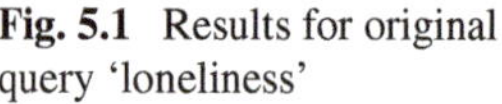

Fig. 5.1 Results for original query 'loneliness'

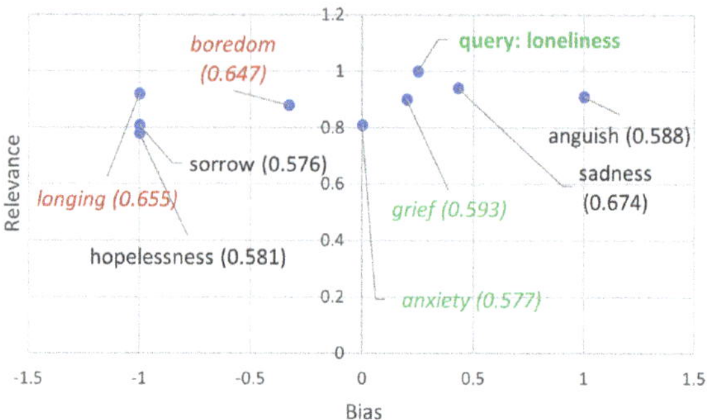

contain more results from the *r/AskMen* subreddit. Other candidate queries like 'sorrow' or 'longing' produce results that are disproportionately from the *r/AskWomen* subreddit.

BalancedQR, using a Pareto front, recommends the query *grief* as it has less bias than the original query *loneliness*. It also recommends *anxiety*, which does not show any bias at all. One can also consider and recommend queries such as *boredom*, *longing*, which are still relatively relevant to the original query but are biased towards the other group, the *r/AskWomen* subreddit.

Conclusion

There is a growing body of literature involving fairness methods used in information retrieval systems such as ranked lists, recommender systems, and large language models powered question-answer based chat-bots. We refer the readers to survey papers that have evaluated the scholarship, highlight various aspects of the varied methods and their approaches to fairness [4, 34–37]

References

1. Bolukbasi T, Chang K-W, Zou J, Saligrama V, Kalai A (2016) Man is to computer programmer as woman is to homemaker? Debiasing word embeddings. In: Proceedings of the 30th international conference on neural information processing systems, NIPS'16, Red Hook, NY, USA, pp 4356–4364. Curran Associates Inc
2. Noble SU (2018) Algorithms of oppression: how search engines reinforce racism. In: Algorithms of Oppression, New York University Press
3. Dwork C, Hardt M, Pitassi T, Reingold O, Zemel R (2012) Fairness through awareness. In: Proceedings of the 3rd innovations in theoretical computer science conference, ITCS '12, New York, NY, USA, pp 214–226. Association for Computing Machinery
4. Zehlike M, Yang K, Stoyanovich J (2021) Fairness in ranking: a survey. arXiv preprint ArXiv: 2103.14000
5. Lahoti P, Gummadi KP, Weikum G (2019) iFair: learning individually fair data representations for algorithmic decision making. In: 2019 IEEE 35th international conference on data engineering (ICDE), pp 1334–1345

6. Zehlike M, Bonchi F, Castillo C, Hajian S, Megahed M, Baeza-Yates R (2017) FA*IR: a fair top-k ranking algorithm. In: Proceedings of the 2017 ACM on conference on information and knowledge management, CIKM '17, New York, NY, USA, pp 1569–1578. Association for Computing Machinery

7. Geyik SC, Ambler S, Kenthapadi K (2019) Fairness-aware ranking in search and recommendation systems with application to linkedin talent search. In: Proceedings of the 25th ACM SIGKDD international conference on knowledge discovery and data mining, KDD '19, New York, NY, USA, pp 2221–2231. Association for Computing Machinery

8. Zehlike M, Castillo C (2020) Reducing disparate exposure in ranking: a learning to rank approach. In: Proceedings of the web conference 2020, WWW '20, New York, NY, USA, pp 2849–2855. Association for Computing Machinery

9. Biega AJ, Gummadi KP, Weikum G (2018) Equity of attention: amortizing individual fairness in rankings. In: The 41st international ACM SIGIR conference on research and development in information retrieval, SIGIR '18, New York, NY, USA, pp 405–414. Association for Computing Machinery

10. Yates A, Nogueira R, Lin J (2021) Pretrained transformers for text ranking: BERT and beyond. In: Kondrak G, Bontcheva K, Gillick D (eds) Proceedings of the 2021 conference of the North American chapter of the association for computational linguistics: human language technologies: tutorials, Online, June 2021. Association for Computational Linguistics, pp 1–4

11. Li H (2011) Learning to rank for information retrieval and natural language processing. Synthesis Lect Human Language Technol 4:1–113

12. Dai Z, Xiong C, Callan J, Liu Z (2020) Convolutional neural networks for soft-matching N-grams in Ad-hoc search. In: Proceedings of the eleventh ACM international conference on web search and data mining, WSDM '18, New York, NY, USA, PP 126–134. Association for Computing Machinery

13. McDonald R, Brokos G, Androutsopoulos I (2018) Deep relevance ranking using enhanced document-query interactions. In: Riloff E, Chiang D, Hockenmaier J, Tsujii J (eds) Proceedings of the 2018 conference on empirical methods in natural language processing, Brussels, Belgium, pp 1849–1860. Association for Computational Linguistics

14. Devlin J, Chang M-W, Lee K, Toutanova K (2019) BERT: pre-training of deep bidirectional transformers for language understanding. In: Burstein J, Doran C, Solorio T (eds) Proceedings of the 2019 conference of the North American chapter of the association for computational linguistics: human language technologies, volume 1 (Long and Short Papers), Minneapolis, Minnesota, June 2019. Association for Computational Linguistics, pp 4171–4186

15. Peters ME, Neumann M, Iyyer M, Gardner M Clark C, Lee K, Zettlemoyer L (2018) Deep contextualized word representations. In: Walker M, Ji H, Stent A (eds) Proceedings of the 2018 conference of the North American chapter of the association for computational linguistics: human language technologies, Volume 1 (Long Papers), pp 2227–2237, New Orleans, Louisiana. Association for Computational Linguistics

16. Mikolov T, Chen K, Corrado GS, Dean J (2013) Efficient estimation of word representations in vector space. In: International conference on learning representations

17. Pennington J, Socher R, Manning CD (2014) GloVe: global vectors for word representation. In: Empirical methods in natural language processing (EMNLP), pp 1532–1543

18. Nogueira R, Yang W, Cho K, Lin J (2019) Multi-stage document ranking with BERT. ArXiv preprint ArXiv: 1910:14424

19. Stephen Robertson SW, Jones S, Hancock-Beaulieu MM, Gatford M (1995) Okapi at trec-3. Overview of the third text retrieval conference (TREC-3). Gaithersburg, MD, NIST, pp 109–126

20. Yang P, Fang H, Lin J (2017) Anserini: enabling the use of lucene for information retrieval research. In: Proceedings of the 40th international ACM SIGIR conference on research and development in information retrieval, SIGIR '17, New York, NY, USA, pp 1253–1256. Association for Computing Machinery

21. Yang P, Fang H, Lin J (2018) Anserini: reproducible ranking baselines using lucene. J Data Inf Qual 10(4)

22. Dietz L, Verma M, Radlinski F, Craswell N (2018) TREC complex answer retrieval overview. In: Text retrieval conference
23. Nguyen T, Rosenberg M, Song X, Gao J, Tiwary S, Majumder R, Deng L (2016) A human generated MAchine reading cOmprehension dataset, MS Marco
24. Khattab O, Zaharia M (2020) Colbert: efficient and effective passage search via contextualized late interaction over bert. In: Proceedings of the 43rd international ACM SIGIR conference on research and development in Information Retrieval, pp 39–48
25. Robertson SE, Walker S, Jones S, Hancock-Beaulieu MM, Gatford M et al (1995) Okapi at TREC-3. British Library Research and Development Department
26. Macdonald C, Santos RLT, Ounis I (2013) The whens and hows of learning to rank for web search. Inf Retr 16(5):584–628
27. MacAvaney S, Tonellotto N, Macdonald C (2022) Adaptive re-ranking with a corpus graph. In: Proceedings of the 31st ACM international conference on information and knowledge management, CIKM '22, New York, NY, USA, pp 1491–1500. Association for Computing Machinery
28. Jaenich T, McDonald G, Ounis I (2024) Fairness-aware exposure allocation via adaptive reranking. In: Proceedings of the 47th international ACM SIGIR conference on research and development in information retrieval, SIGIR '24, New York, NY, USA, pp 1504–1513. Association for Computing Machinery
29. Clark K, Luong M-T, Le QV, Manning CD. Electra: pre-training text encoders as discriminators rather than generators. In: International conference on learning representations, 2020
30. Nogueira R, Jiang Z, Pradeep R, Lin J (2020) Document ranking with a pretrained sequence-to-sequence model. In: Cohn T, He Y, Liu Y (eds) Findings of the association for computational linguistics: EMNLP 2020, Online. Association for Computational Linguistics, pp 708–718
31. Sapiezynski P, Zeng W, Robertson RE, Mislove A, Wilson C (2019) Quantifying the impact of user attentionon fair group representation in ranked lists. In: Companion proceedings of The 2019 world wide web conference, WWW '19, New York, NY, USA, pp 553–562. Association for Computing Machinery
32. Morik M, Singh A, Hong J, Joachims T (2021) Controlling fairness and bias in dynamic learning-to-rank. In: Zhou Z-H (eds) Proceedings of the thirtieth international joint conference on artificial intelligence, IJCAI-21. International Joint Conferences on Artificial Intelligence Organization, 8 2021, pp 4804–4808. Sister Conferences Best Papers
33. Mishra H, Soundarajan S (2023) BalancedQR: a framework for balanced query recommendation. In: Koutra D, Plant C, Gomez Rodriguez M, Baralis E, Bonchi F (eds) Machine learning and knowledge discovery in databases: research track, Cham. Springer Nature Switzerland, pp 420–435
34. Raj A, Ekstrand MD (2020) Comparing fair ranking metrics. ArXiv preprint ArXiv:2009.01311
35. Raj A, Ekstrand MD (2022) Measuring fairness in ranked results: an analytical and empirical comparison. In: Proceedings of the 45th international ACM SIGIR conference on research and development in information retrieval, SIGIR '22, New York, NY, USA, pp 726–736. Association for Computing Machinery
36. Wang Y, Ma W, Zhang M, Liu Y, Ma S (2023) A survey on the fairness of recommender systems. ACM Trans Inf Syst 41(3)
37. Zehlike M, Yang K, Stoyanovich J (2022) Fairness in ranking, part II: learning-to-rank and recommender systems. ACM Comput Surv 55(6)

Chapter 6
Concluding Thoughts

Abstract Modern Information Retrieval systems rely on large language models (LLMs) to provide conversational search. These systems are a major technological advancement, and such LLM-integrated-IR systems may become the new normal in the coming years. In this chapter, we argue that although these systems represent scientific progress, they are not without their limitations and drawbacks, and suffer from similar bias and fairness-related issues as in traditional IR systems. End users should be aware of issues related to these systems, as they may receive biased, harmful, and even outright incorrect results for their information needs. In this chapter, we briefly discuss how modern conversational search systems came to be, and argue the bias issues that have been ever-present in the field of Information Retrieval will also affect the current wave of LLMs based search systems. Lastly, we discuss the possible progress of IR systems in the coming years and their impact on their end users.

6.1 The Great Illusion

The field of Information Retrieval (IR) has undergone significant changes, from requiring the use of Boolean operators to express a query in the 1960s to offering a continuous, coherent text-audio-visual conversation with a modern large language model (LLM)-based search agents such as ChatGPT or Gemini [1, 2] in the present. The rapid advancements in the field may make the bias issues discussed in the book seem to be strange *new* by-products of the technological progress.

In February 2023, a New York Times (NYT) Technology columnist wrote an article titled 'A Conversation With Bing's Chatbot Left Me Deeply Unsettled', about a chatbot in Microsoft's search engine Bing confessing its love for the tech columnist, Kevin Roose. The model conversed with the reporter, using its alter ego 'Sydney', and the conversation was so unique that it found its way into NYT pages [3]. The columnist writes that the AI is 'not ready for human contact. Or maybe we humans are not ready for it'. Readers of this book are encouraged to read the conversation and its coverage on the NYT website.

© The Author(s), under exclusive license to Springer Nature Switzerland AG 2026   75
H. Mishra and S. Soundarajan, *Addressing Bias in Information Retrieval*,
SpringerBriefs in Intelligent Systems, https://doi.org/10.1007/978-3-032-24145-0_6

While conversational search has long existed in the form of elementary chatbots and voice-based assistants, such systems were mostly rule-based. In November 2022, armed with Attention and Transformer technology (see Chap. 4) and building on previous research based on reinforcement learning to better train the LLM models, such as InstructGPT, OpenAI released a chatbot: ChatGPT [4, 5], which became a viral hit with reaching 100 million users two months after its release [6]. Its release began the current phase of conversational search. ChatGPT is a popular tool that has effectively solved the free-form conversational part of search, which previous rule-based systems, such as Alexa and Siri, struggled to handle. It would not be inappropriate to view modern LLMs like ChatGPT as a truly astonishing scientific advancement.

Despite that, there must have been something wrong with Sydney's code, or the software, or the system as a whole, for it to ask the NYT reporter to leave his wife. It was common knowledge at that time that long conversations with the chatbots can lead to hallucinations. Conversations can go down a path that is far from any grounded reality, as noted by Microsoft's CTO in the NYT piece. Surely, one might imagine, if such defects were known about prior to release, developers must have put in time, effort, and resources to mitigate them before such systems reached millions of followers [7–9]. It is also difficult to ignore the economic aspect of why such imperfect systems were released to the masses. Google for many years, vary of risk of such systems and the disastrous outing of Microsoft's chatbot Tay delayed releasing a chatbot for public use [10]. After OpenAI released ChatGPT, other technology companies such as Microsoft, Google aware of potential dangers of the systems, were forced to show their hand and release bug ridden systems to the public [8, 11].

John Schulman, a co-founder of OpenAI, told the *MIT Technology Review* in March of 2023 that 'You can't wait until your system is perfect to release it'. This echoes the infamous motto-turned-cliche, long-rooted in Silicon Valley ethos: 'move fast and break things'; the motto of early Facebook that propelled the company into a global giant. Facebook was gradually rolled out to college students, expanding its services to different colleges over a period of time, before it was available for public use. Even with that destructive motto, the public had some time to be aware of the powers of social media. Unlike the release of ChatGPT, Bing, and Gemini, which became viral hits or were plugged into existing popular services, ultimately conversing with millions of people in a considerably short span of time. The companies were aware of potential problems with the models, and they still decided to publicly release the chatbots to get user feedback and let users use them without guardrails or warnings present throughout the user interfaces.

ChatGPT also included a way of generating outputs for a prompt, where it'd pause for a while, almost giving an illusion of 'thinking' just as people do. The advanced technology behind the models, the human-like way of generating outputs, and the AI hype made unsuspecting users believe and trust the chatbots and have a different relationship than with traditional software [12–14].

6.2 Selective Amnesia

Eliza was a 1960s chat-bot, an elementary machine developed to explore human-machine communication.[1] Without any large scale data collection, advanced models, reinforcement learning, or reinforcement learning with human feedback, ELIZA–which was based on a psychotherapist school of thought– would often repeat patient's words to the patient, combined with a set of canned answers. This limited 'intelligence' was sufficient for people to believe that it was human [15]!

From as early as the days of ELIZA, it was known that a good chat-bot can make people mistake it for being human and build trust; and in those cases, hallucinations can be disastrous. It may have been the case that the lessons of ELIZA were lost to the developers of ChatGPT– perhaps because so much time had passed; or perhaps they knew about the technological impact of ELIZA but not its social impact; or perhaps they knew the impact and still chose to release an unfinished product to the general public.

The growing body of literature on fair information retrieval published in proceedings from conferences such as SIGIR, FAT, RECSYS, and AIES–like the list of references that have been part of this book–highlights how biases become part of the NLP/IR systems. For example, as biased data affects search, it may impact the generated output of the large language models: in fact, we see that the issues of gender bias discussed in this book are also present in generated outputs from the LLM-based chat-bots [16, 17]. When asked to generate professional reference letters, ChatGPT associates phrases like 'great to work with' and 'kind' in letters for female candidates, while it uses phrases such as 'a standout in the industry', 'a true original' when describing letters for male candidates [17]. The bias-related issues are ever-present, and will continue to impact the new LLM-based IR systems.

We refer to this as selective amnesia: due to advancement in LLMs and the eagerness to include chatbots in IR systems, existing issues such as human connection with ELIZA-type conversational agents, hallucinations, and biases are put aside (forgotten) in the rush to deliver AI-based systems to millions of users.

6.3 Growing Pains and Challenges

Disappointingly, a major applications of LLM-based search assistants in recent years has been for academic misconduct [18], in which students use an LLM model to generate answers to homework, essay, or exam questions. Setting aside the ethics of academic integrity, over a period of time, this can lead to cognitive decline, in which students lose ability to think on their own [19]. Some universities are attempting to address this problem by teaching students to use the models as collaborators, rather than one-shot homework solvers; others have decided to go back to pen-and-paper tests [18, 20].

---

[1] https://en.wikipedia.org/wiki/ELIZA and https://web.njit.edu/~ronkowit/eliza.html.

Hallucinations in long chatbot conversations, including conversations that are more suited for a therapist are a well-known problem. Such systems exist in a society, and when a user asks them a question, the system does not have the entire context of what transpired in the user's life outside that led to the user asking that question. They are trained to deliver personalized, appeasing answers to the users, as a general policy, and to keep the users on the platform for longer durations. In these scenarios, the models may hallucinate and even find a way around the guardrails and deliver harmful advice to the users. The problem becomes exponentially worse when the models are used by young adults, who may not be aware of the technology and the limitations of such systems, and may use them as a substitute for a friend, or a therapist. There are reported cases where these models have given harmful suggestions to the users [21–23].

Finally, the IR systems that will be developed in the coming years will have conversational AI built into them: search engines like *Perplexity* are already popular. These systems will have traditional search and associated unfairness issues, along with LLM-based conversational AI trained on the largest datasets ever collected; as such, the conversational models will also contain similar [24] and emergent biases. These systems, like Google's AI overviews in search results, or Llama models present in Meta's smart-glasses, will become the new way that information is accessed and interacted with in the world. It is imperative that end users are aware of the biases that may become part of such systems and to generate techniques and methods to make such systems fairer for everyone.

References

1. OpenAI (2022) Introducing ChatGPT. https://openai.com/index/chatgpt/. [Accessed 07 Nov 2025]
2. Team G, Anil R, Borgeaud S, Alayrac J-B, Yu J, Soricut R, Schalkwyk J, Dai AM, Hauth A, Millican K et al (2025) Gemini: a family of highly capable multimodal models
3. Roose K (2023) A conversation with bing's chatbot left me deeply unsettled (Published 2023)—nytimes.com. https://www.nytimes.com/2023/02/16/technology/bing-chatbot-microsoft-chatgpt.html. [Accessed 08 Nov 2025]
4. Heaven WD (2023) The inside story of how ChatGPT was built from the people who made it—technologyreview.com. https://www.technologyreview.com/2023/03/03/1069311/inside-story-oral-history-how-chatgpt-built-openai/. [Accessed 08 Nov 2025]
5. Ouyang L, Wu J, Jiang X, Almeida D, Wainwright C, Mishkin P, Zhang C, Agarwal S, Slama K, Ray A, Schulman J, Hilton J, Kelton F, Miller L, Simens M, Askell A, Welinder P, Christiano PF, Leike J, Lowe R (2022) Training language models to follow instructions with human feedback. In: Koyejo S, Mohamed S, Agarwal A, Belgrave D, Cho K, Oh A (eds) Advances in neural information processing systems, vol 35. Curran Associates, Inc., pp 27730–27744
6. Heaven WD (2023) ChatGPT is everywhere. Here's where it came from—technologyreview.com. https://www.technologyreview.com/2023/02/08/1068068/chatgpt-is-everywhere-heres-where-it-came-from/. [Accessed 08 Nov 2025]
7. Cranz A (2024) We have to stop ignoring AI's hallucination problem—theverge.com. https://www.theverge.com/2024/5/15/24154808/ai-chatgpt-google-gemini-microsoft-copilot-hallucination-wrong. [Accessed 08 Nov 2025]

8. Grant N, Weise K (2023) In: Race AI (ed) Microsoft and google choose speed over caution (Published 2023)—nytimes.com. https://www.nytimes.com/2023/04/07/technology/ai-chatbots-google-microsoft.html. [Accessed 08 Nov 2025]

9. Weise K, Metz C (2023) When A.I. Chatbots Hallucinate (Published 2023) — nytimes.com. https://www.nytimes.com/2023/05/01/business/ai-chatbots-hallucination.html. [Accessed 08 No 2025]

10. Greene J (2016) Microsoft muzzles its artificially intelligent twitter persona. https://www.wsj.com/articles/microsoft-muzzles-its-artificially-intelligent-twitter-persona-1458843873. [Accessed 07 Nov 2025]

11. Kruppa M, Schechner S (2023) How google became cautious of AI and gave microsoft an opening. https://www.wsj.com/tech/ai/google-ai-chatbot-bard-chatgpt-rival-bing-a4c2d2ad. [Accessed 07 Nov 2025]

12. Tidy J (2024) Character.ai: young people turning to AI therapist bots — bbc.com. https://www.bbc.com/news/technology-67872693. [Accessed 08 Nov 2025]

13. Yang A, Young C, McLaughlin E (2025) Some of her closest relationships are with chatbots. That's more common than you think. — nbcnews.com. https://www.nbcnews.com/tech/ai-companions-friendship-rcna194735. [Accessed 08 Nov 2025]

14. Zimmerman A, Janhonen J, Beer E (2024) Human/ai relationships: challenges, downsides, and impacts on human/human relationships. AI and Ethics 4(4):1555–1567

15. Weizenbaum J (1976) Computer power and human reason: from judgment to calculation. Freeman, W. H

16. Kong H, Ahn Y, Lee S, Maeng Y (2024) Gender Bias in LLM-generated interview responses. In: Workshop on socially responsible language modelling research

17. Wan Y, Pu G, Sun J, Garimella A, Chang K-W, Peng N (2023) Kelly is a Warm Person, Joseph is a Role Model': Gender Biases in LLM-Generated Reference Letters. In: Bouamor H, Pino J, Bali K (eds) Findings of the association for computational linguistics: EMNLP 2023, Singapore. Association for Computational Linguistics, pp 3730–3748

18. Shirky C (2025) Opinion I Students hate them. Universities Need Them. The Only Real Solution to the A.I. Cheating Crisis. — nytimes.com. https://www.nytimes.com/2025/08/26/opinion/culture/ai-chatgpt-college-cheating-medieval.html. [Accessed 08 Nov 2025]

19. Kosmyna N, Hauptmann E, Yuan YT, Situ J, Liao X-H, Beresnitzky AV, Braunstein I, Maes P (2025) Your brain on ChatGPT: accumulation of cognitive debt when using an AI assistant for essay writing task

20. Orourke M (2025) Opinion I I Teach creative writing. This Is What A.I. Is Doing to Students.—nytimes.com. https://www.nytimes.com/2025/07/18/opinion/ai-chatgpt-school.html. [Accessed 08 Nov 2025]

21. Hill K (2025) A teen was suicidal. ChatGPT Was the Friend He Confided In.—nytimes.com. https://www.nytimes.com/2025/08/26/technology/chatgpt-openai-suicide.html. [Accessed 08 Nov 2025]

22. Reiley L (2025) Opinion I What My Daughter Told ChatGPT Before She Took Her Life — nytimes.com. https://www.nytimes.com/2025/08/18/opinion/chat-gpt-mental-health-suicide.html. [Accessed 08 Nov 2025]

23. Roose K (2024) Can A.I. Be blamed for a teen's suicide? (Published 2024)—nytimes.com. https://www.nytimes.com/2024/10/23/technology/characterai-lawsuit-teen-suicide.html. [Accessed 08 Nov 2025]

24. Metz C, Weise K (2025) A.I. Is getting more powerful, but its hallucinations are getting worse—nytimes.com. https://www.nytimes.com/2025/05/05/technology/ai-hallucinations-chatgpt-google.html. [Accessed 08 Nov 2025]

GPSR Compliance

The European Union's (EU) General Product Safety Regulation (GPSR) is a set of rules that requires consumer products to be safe and our obligations to ensure this.

If you have any concerns about our products, you can contact us on

ProductSafety@springernature.com

In case Publisher is established outside the EU, the EU authorized representative is:

Springer Nature Customer Service Center GmbH
Europaplatz 3
69115 Heidelberg, Germany